THE

NIMROD

THE

NIMROD

MIGHTY HUNTER

ANDY EVANS

DALRYMPLE
& VERDUN◆
PUBLISHING

The Nimrod
Mighty Hunter
Andy Evans

ISBN 978-1-905414-06-2

First published in 2007 by
Dalrymple & Verdun Publishing
33 Adelaide Street
Stamford
Lincolnshire
PE9 2EN
United Kingdom
Tel: 0845 838 1940
mail@dvpublishing.co.uk
www.dvpublishing.co.uk

© Concept and design
Dalrymple & Verdun Publishing and
Stephen Thompson Associates
© Andy Evans 2006
Editor and commissioning editor
Martin Derry
© Richard J Caruana colour profiles

The right of Andy Evans to be identified
as the author of this work has been
asserted in accordance with sections 77
and 78 of the Copyright Designs and
Patents Act, 1988.

Printed in England by
Ian Allan Printing Limited
Riverdene Business Park
Molesey Road
Hersham
Surrey
KT12 4RG

Half title: *Nimrod MRA.4 ZJ518
previously MR.2 XV234.*
BAe Systems

Title page: *MR.2P XV260 over the
Highlands of Scotland.* RAF Kinloss

Opposite page: *An outstanding
image of RAF Kinloss, Scotland,
the principle base of the maritime
Nimrods.* RAF Kinloss

CONTENTS

ACKNOWLEDGMENTS
Thanks are due to all who have freely provided
information and photographs for this book.
However, special thanks are due to the following:
Gordon Bartley, long time friend and goldmine
for photographic information, Mathew Clements,
Chris Muir, Dale Donovan RAFPR, BAE Systems
Warton, Dawn McNiven at RAF Kinloss, RAF
Waddington and the individual Nimrod units.

Photographs credited to 'Andy Evans
Collection' have either been taken by the author
or form part of a collection from various sources,
and in some cases the original photographers
names are not known. However, there is no
intention to breach any individual copyright and
the author would be pleased to hear from
anyone whose image is represented in this book
but not credited accordingly.

The publishers would like to thank the
following for their invaluable contribution: Terry
Senior, Tim Senior, Trevor Snowden of Hornby
Hobbies Limited for their photographs, Chris
Salter, and Dennis Robinson for his assistance
regarding the Nimrod colour schemes.

Chapter 1: **GENESIS TO MIGHTY HUNTER – PROTOTYPES, MR.1 AND MR.2**

As an Island Nation Great Britain has historically been a keen defender of her shores and coastal waters. Having suffered horrendous losses to its merchant navy and Royal Naval shipping in two world wars, the UK appreciates more than most the need to keep watch on vessels both on and under the surface in the waters that encircle it. Since the end of World War II many of the demands of this vital patrolling had fallen on the shoulders of the noisy, uncomfortable, but much loved piston engined Avro Shackleton maritime reconnaissance aircraft. With the Cold War reaching its height, a successor was needed for the Shackleton, a new breed of aircraft that had endurance, comfort, speed if necessary, and above all modern sea search equipment in order to counter the increasingly sophisticated threats of the twentieth-century. What emerged from this requirement was, and perhaps still

Avro Shackleton MR.2A WL754 overflying RAF Finningley Yorkshire in September 1965. WL754 was later converted to become an AEW.2 and was withdrawn from service in January 1981. Newark Air Museum

Opposite top: De Havilland Comet T.2 XK669 Taurus of 216 Squadron RAF. XK669 was later converted to become a C.2 and was struck off charge in April 1966 and scrapped at Brize Norton the following year. Newark Air Museum

Opposite bottom: Comet C.4 XR399 of 216 Squadron. XR399 served with this unit from February 1962 until approximately June 1975. It became G-BDIX on 1st September 1975. Newark Air Museum

is the greatest jet powered maritime aircraft of all time, the Hawker Siddeley (later BAe) Nimrod. The Nimrod offered significant advantages of speed and height during transit, whilst still capable of long patrol periods and, in particular, stealth in the anti-submarine mission as propeller-engined aircraft produce a discrete resonance that can be detected by submerged submarines whereas the jet noise of the Nimrod is virtually undetectable.

Named after the 'mighty hunter' described in the Bible, the Nimrod has successfully patrolled the seas around the British Isles for more than three decades. The Nimrod story proper begins in 1957 when British aircraft manufacturers began to take an interest in a NATO competition for a maritime reconnaissance aircraft to replace the Lockheed Neptune, and saw an opening for a new aircraft to undertake the task for the RAF. Avro had discussions with Breguet who won the

NATO contract with their twin turbo-prop Tyne powered Atlantic 2A, and the two firms jointly proposed a modified Atlantic, the Avro-Breguet 2A, with two additional RB.153-61 jet engines fitted on under-wing pylons and wing tip fuel tanks. This came to nothing when Avro couldn't agree with Breguet's use of honeycomb for the fuselage shell, and when an abortive attempt to find a NATO standard Maritime Patrol Aircraft had failed in 1959, the UK made a renewed attempt to replace the Avro Shackleton in the maritime patrol role when, in July of 1963, Air Staff Target (AST) 357 was issued. This called for a sophisticated medium sized jet powered aircraft to undertake the Anti Submarine Warfare and Coastal Patrol duty. This aircraft was required to have three or more engines (jet or turbo-prop), transit to the operational area at a speed of 400 knots or better, and loiter for approximately eight hours thereafter. Proposals submitted included the HS.800, a three engined jet design based on the Hawker Siddeley Trident, a BAC 10-11 (a version of the 1-11 airliner with VC-10 wings), a project called the Avro 776 (a four-engined version of the 748), and fast and slow versions of the Short Belfast freighter. However, the estimated costs involved in developing such aircraft proved much too high. The Avro 776 appeared to be the likely winner, but on 19th June 1964 the RAF issued a new requirement, Air Staff Requirement (ASR) 381 and this called for a much less capable aircraft, but one which would match or exceed the performance of the French Breguet Atlantic.

The Avro team (by now part of Hawker Siddeley) was stunned and in an attempt to prevent the French aircraft from winning the contest, it took them just seven days for their engineers to produce a design for a 'new' aircraft using an existing airframe with its associated tooling, existing production engines, and still retain the required high speed and long endurance. This concept, based on the already available De Havilland Comet 4 wings and fuselage and married to the Rolls-Royce RB.168 engine, became known as the HS.801. This new design involved mating the proven Comet airframe, already in service with RAF Transport Command with an under fuselage pannier similar to the one developed for the HS.800 proposal, thereby giving the aircraft a larger equipment area and room for expansion of new systems. This pannier was the essential element of the Nimrod design and would turn a benign airliner into a powerful submarine hunter-killer. The panniers' dimensions were determined by the equipment the RAF needed to carry within, and its shape was further governed by basic aerodynamic principles. The new fuselage shape

therefore was created first to house the air-to-surface vessel ASV-21 radar scanner, and then, looking ahead, it was to accommodate the proposed Search-water scanner, plus a Doppler aerial bay and of course, a weapons bay. In a very short space of time, Hawker Siddeley had developed an unpressurised lower fuselage fairing which fitted around the lower portion of the aircraft, giving it a distinctive 'double-bubble' shape. Extending from the nose to the rear fuselage this pannier brought a dramatic increase in useable space for operational equipment and weapons whilst minimising additional drag, and endowed the aircraft with a unique profile. By replacing the Comet's existing Rolls-Royce Avon engines with new, less-thirsty, military Mk 250 RB.168-200 Spey turbofans, a very acceptable endurance was achieved. Designated HS.801, the Comet derivative was offered to meet ASR 381 in the July of 1964. Subsequently in February 1965 it was announced in Parliament that the HS.801 or 'Maritime Comet' had been selected to replace the Shackleton, and prior to that event a 'maritime profile' assessment sortie had been flown in late April 1964 in a Comet 3 from Hatfield with Hawker Siddeley designers on board to assess the 'project's' potential. A fixed price contract for 38 production aircraft was agreed in January 1966, at which time the name 'Nimrod' was selected. In the meantime, the conversion of two unsold Comet 4C airframes which were to act as prototypes had begun.

Conversion work on the first development prototype, XV148 started at the Hawker Siddeley factory near Chester early in 1966 using an unfinished Comet airframe which had the manufacturer's construction number 6477. Because this airframe had not been fully assembled when the project began it was easier to install the Spey engines from the outset and became the first 'Nimrod' to fly, albeit a mere 40 miles from Chester to Woodford in the hands of John Cun-

ningham on 23rd May 1967. The second Nimrod prototype was XV147, a Comet 4C with the manufacturers number 6467, which retained its Rolls-Royce Avon engines and first flew on 31st July 1967.

Following the Comet airliner disasters of 1953 and 1954, and the painstaking work which went into discovering the causes, the Comet had become one of the most reliable and best-liked passenger aircraft in the world, indeed the RAF also embraced the Comet, equipping No.216 Squadron in mid 1956. No.216 Squadron thus became the world's first military jet transport unit receiving 10 Comet 2s (2xT.2 [later converted to C.2] and 8xC.2). This squadron also received five Comet C.4s (the militarised version of the Comet 4C), from February 1962 these latter remaining in service until June 1975 affording the RAF some relevant experience toward flying and maintaining the Nimrod. Additionally No. 51 Squadron RAF also operated the Comet (R.2 and C.2) from 1958 until gradually replaced by the Nimrod R.1 from 1971. It may be noted of course that several non-standard Comets sporting many and various modifications served as trials or research aircraft with the various British test and evaluation units over many years.

Nimrod MR.1

It was soon clear that Nimrod had the 'right stuff' to become a successful maritime patrol aircraft. It had a payload capacity of approximately 23,000lb, sufficiently able to cope with the anti-submarine warfare equipment, weapons and large crew complement; it boasted a comfortable ride, a healthy 'dash' with an ability to loiter at medium speed and an excellent extended range. Anyone taking a cursory glance at XV148 at its initial roll out may be forgiven if their first impression was that of it merely being a Comet 4C with a bulge underneath. There was of course, far more to it than that, as Nimrod really was essentially a new

Comet 4C XS235 Canopus seen at RAF Mildenhall, Suffolk in May 1988. Not part of the RAF inventory but used by the RAE/DERA until 1997. It was the last military Comet in service prior to retirement to Bruntingthorpe airfield in Leicestershire, where it has acquired the civil registration of G-CPDA and is currently maintained in taxiable condition.
Martin Derry

Spey-engined prototype XV148 in its MR.1 guise, at this stage waiting to be fitted with its distinctive Magnetic Anomaly Detector (MAD) boom. The fin fillet was increased in size at a later date, comparison with the photograph below shows the extent of the increase. The engine nacelles and wing roots appear to be unpainted, perhaps they were replacement panels. The weapons bay doors are shown slightly ajar. Gordon Bartley

At a slightly later date XV148 has obviously received a new colour scheme and the larger fin fillet but is still without a MAD boom. Most, if not all of the original windows were retained on XV147 and XV148 following their conversion from the Comet 4C, the quantity of windows make an interesting comparison with production Nimrods. Photographs would suggest that XV148 was never fitted with a search light. Chris Muir

design rather than a conversion to a new role. The Nimrod's appearance, in comparison with the Comet, was further altered following the installation of the pannier which had created directional instability, thus requiring a redesign of the dorsal fin area and the introduction of a fin fillet during June 1967. At the same time the curved glass fibre Electronic Surveillance Measures (ESM) aerial fairing on the fin top was also added. Surprisingly, the Nimrods were in fact six feet shorter from nose to rudder than the Comet 4Cs, a section having been taken out of the fuselage immediately ahead of the wing with a view to this further improving directional stability. A long tail boom was added which was required to house the submarine detecting ASQ-10A MAD (Magnetic Anomaly Detector) which also positioned the aerial as far away from the metallic mass of the aircraft as possible. Noticeable was the larger intake areas demanded by the Spey engines. The outer engines were fitted with thrust reverse which when selected diverted the exhaust gases diagonally from cascade ports above and below the engine fairings thus allowing for a shorter landing run if required. Further changes included the pilots' windscreen being deepened to improve visibility at low level and 'eyebrow' windows added to assist the crew to 'look' into the tight turns expected in anti-submarine warfare flying. Two of the wing ribs were strengthened to carry weapon pylons, and indeed at one stage of development, Martel air-to-surface (ASM) weapons were fitted and tested and other munitions contemplated; an option not used until the Falklands War in 1982 when Sidewinder air-to-air missiles (AAM) were fitted. A 70 million candle power Strong Electric searchlight was incorporated into the starboard external wing tank for search and rescue duties controlled from the cockpit, and the undercarriage strengthened from that of the Comet 4C to cope with potential increases in all-up weights.

The MR.1 carried a crew of 14 including, two pilots, a flight engineer, navigator, tactical navigator, radio operator, radar operator, two sonar operators, an electronic counter measures operator (ECM), a Magnetic Anomaly detector (MAD) operator, two surveillance operators and cargo master. The sonar system, fitted in the rear of the aircraft, dealt with the release of sonar buoys, and for anti-submarine tasks the MR.1 could accommodate up to nine torpedoes. For use against surface targets free fall bombs could be carried. The principle sensor was the ASV 21 radar set,

MR.1 XV230 making a low pass over RAF St.Athan in the early 1970s. Sadly this is the aircraft that crashed in southern Kandahar on 9th September 2006 with the loss of all 14 persons on board.
Andy Evans Collection

but from the outset this was always intended to be replaced by the more capable Searchwater radar unit when it became available. The ASV 21 could detect large ships up to a distance of 150 nautical miles, vessels of less than 100 tons at 40 nautical miles, surfaced submarines at 75 nautical miles and 'snorting' submarines at 20 nautical miles. It could be operated at full power up to an altitude of 40,000ft and could be used to detect landmasses at the maximum range of its Plan Position Indicator (PPI) display – about 170 nautical miles, and additionally could be used for cloud collision warning and as a navigation aid.

Following the prototypes, the first true HS.801 Nimrod flew in June 1968 bearing the airframe number XV226. It and XV227, XV228 and XV229 became the production development aircraft, all later entering RAF service under the service designation of Nimrod MR.1. In all there were to be five operational Nimrod squadrons and one training unit, and these would be based in Malta, southwest England and Scotland. The first MR.1 to enter RAF service was XV230 with the Maritime Operational Training Unit (later becoming No.236 Operational Conversion Unit on 1st July 1970) at RAF St.Mawgan in Cornwall on 2nd October 1969, arriving just in time to line up behind nine Shackleton's in the fly-past ceremony on 27th November marking the disbandment of Coastal Command and the creation of No 18 (Maritime) Group of the new RAF Strike Command. The remaining 33 air-

craft in the first order for 38 were numbered XV231-XV263 and all but one were delivered on schedule by 31st January 1972, with the last reaching the RAF a little late in August of that year because of an industrial dispute. A further order for an additional eight aircraft was placed in January 1972 and delivery of these began three years later. Only five of them entered service as MR.1's however, as two of them, XZ286 and XZ287, were held and stored for the AEW.3 programme, and XZ284 was built directly to MR.2 standard. The five which did enter squadron service as MR.1's were XZ280 to XZ283 and XZ285. In addition three 'specials' were built for electronic reconnaissance duties with No.51 Squadron, XW664, XW665 and XW666. They were delivered by 1973 to replace the Comet R.2s used by the squadron, and are dealt with in chapter two. Worthy of mention here as part of the Nimrod development programme is XV814, (ex Comet 4C G-APDF) which had been bought for use with the Royal Aircraft Establishment (RAE) in 1967. She was destined to become the last but one airworthy Comet in the world, the last being XS235 Canopus. XV814 became one of the RAE non-standard Comets, initially fitted with 'canoe' fairings of various lengths to house experimental equipment. It was also fitted with a Nimrod fin and rudder to counter the extra keel area of the 'canoes'. By 1977 the aircraft had earned the nickname 'Comrod' and was resplendent in the wonderful 'raspberry ripple' colour scheme evolved by the RAE as a high visibility aid, whilst retaining the elegance of the aircraft.

RAF Kinloss was to receive the first operational Nimrod on 25th June 1970, after which date 120, 201 and 206 Squadrons began conversion. Deliveries to No.42 Squadron at St.Mawgan, occurred in April 1971, with No.203 Squadron commencing conversion on the Nimrod in July 1971, receiving its first aircraft the following October. No.203 Squadron was stationed at Luqa, Malta. All five squadrons had previously operated the Shackleton.

Meanwhile, as mentioned earlier, an order for a second batch of eight MR.1s was announced in January 1972 in order that the existing Nimrod squadrons could be brought up to full strength. During this early period the MR.1 wore a colour scheme of white over Light Aircraft Grey, to suit the overwater roles they undertook. Of the prototypes and development aircraft, XV148 was employed on conversion to Searchwater radar development work, whilst XV147 spent its entire life in research and development of the mission equipment for both the MR.1 and MR.2 versions, although it remained an 'odd-ball', by still retaining Avon engines. Even so, XV147 would play its part in the development of the MRA.4 flight deck mock-ups! Other aircraft used for testing included XV226, the first aircraft to be fully equipped to MR.1 standard and used for the development of engineering systems inside the aircraft, including air conditioning. This aircraft finally entered RAF service as an MR.2 at Kinloss.

Above: *The first production MR.1 XV226, (although not the first MR.1 to enter RAF service). Note the highly polished engine intakes!*
Andy Evans Collection

Below: *MR.1 XZ282 was amongst the last of the MR.1s to enter service, and would later be converted as part of the ill fated AEW.3 programme. This aircraft lacks the black nose of XV226 above.*
Andy Evans Collection

Above: *MR.1 XZ282 lands at Kinloss on an unknown date.* Chris Muir

Right: *MR.1 XV242 at RAF Scampton, Lincolnshire, on 7th June 1980.* Terry Senior

Below right: *MR.1 XV250 at RAF Waddington, Lincolnshire, in May 1980.* Terry Senior

Opposite page:

Top: *A typical scene in the late 1970's as Nimrod XZ280 overflies a Soviet aircraft carrier in the North Sea.*

Bottom: *MR.1 XV231 seen whilst in landing configuration.* Both RAF Kinloss

XV228 was initially a Boscombe Down aircraft used for the A&AEE's assessment of the navigational and NAV/TAC systems, and also for weapon system trials in the Bahamas at the Atlantic Underwater Test & Evaluation Centre (AUTEC). This aircraft entered RAF service on 6th June 1973, after 852 hours test flying. XV229 was another 'oddball' as it was initially used for clearance of all the communications systems, later becoming Boscombe Down's development 'hack' before later entering RAF service as an MR.2.

The first detection of a submerged Soviet nuclear submarine by the RAF occurred on 30th August 1970, when a Nimrod flying out of RAF St.Mawgan located a 'November' class hunter-killer, and the Nimrod soon began proving its worth in its military capacity, as well as becoming a great asset for civilian search and rescue co-ordination duties. The 1974 defence cuts resulted in Malta-based No.203 Squadron being disbanded on 31st December 1977 and it's Nimrods flown back to the UK and placed in storage. In 1975 work commenced on a comprehensive avionics upgrade for the MR.1, and thirty-five aircraft were scheduled to be upgraded to the new MR.2 standard, with the first aircraft being redelivered to No.201 Squadron on 23rd August 1979. It should be remembered that the Nimrod in its MR.1 form was, from its inception, seen as an interim aircraft and that conversion to the better equipped MR.2 standard was envisaged from the outset, the dimensions of the fore end of the pannier having been dictated by the size of the Searchwater radar due to be fitted on the MR.2. The Kinloss wing disposed of its final MR.1 in October 1982 and began working up on the MR.2 in the June of 1983.

Nimrod MR.2

The pre-planned conversion of the 35 aircraft to MR.2 standard began in April 1975 and took rather more than nine years to complete. The conversions required approximately 11 months per aircraft with an average of seven aircraft at any given time being out of RAF service and undergoing modification at Woodford. The vast majority of changes were internal, concerning the tactical and navigation equipment and weapons provision, but externally the most striking difference was the colour scheme. Whilst some early MR.2s retained the grey and white of the MR.1, later conversions received the new NATO Hemp, BS 381C 389 and Light Aircraft Grey BS 381C 627 camouflage colours, thus giving the aircraft a less visible 'flatter' appearance. As the earlier airframes went through major servicing they too emerged wearing the new colours. Other external differences included new aerial arrangements, an additional air scoop on the port side just below the dorsal fin, the disappearance of one cabin window, and wingtip Loral ARI18240 Yellow Gate Electronic Surveillance Measure (ESM) pods fitted as standard. These pods contain several spiral helix aerials for

reception from (all directions) of unknown or hostile signals. Each of these passive receivers is tuned to one wavelength, to aid in the detection of signals communications. Perhaps the most dramatic addition was the incorporation of an ex-Vulcan in-flight refuelling probe as a result of experience gained during the Falklands War (dealt with separately). This necessitated the addition of three auxiliary fins, one under the fuselage and one on each tailplane to cope with yaw stability following the installation of the cabin mounted roof probe. The probe-equipped aircraft were designated MR.2P. Internally the equipment upgrade included a new Marconi GEC central tactical system, based on a new FM1600D computer and three separate 920ATC processors for navigation systems, radar and acoustic sensors. The old ASV-21D radar was replaced by a Thorn EMI ARI5980 Searchwater set, a quantum leap over the former, and now incorporates a colour display. Other additions included a Sandpiper infra-red detection system and a Missile Alert Warning System coupled with wing mounted chaff and flare dispensers. The new Searchwater radar system could now distinguish between ships, and the periscope of a submarine even at its greatest operational range, a huge improvement in detection and classification capability. The acoustics system is based on the AQS901 sonar system, compatible with BARRA, SSQ-41 and SSQ-53, TANDEM, and Ultra active and passive sonobuoys. Communications equipment was upgraded and included two AS470 radio and encryption systems. Nimrod prototype XV147 was converted to the new MR.2 standard, albeit retaining her Avon engines, and was the first in the programme to fly to the new MR.2 specification, the first flight taking place in April 1977. Nimrod XV236 became the first true MR.2 to enter service on 23rd August 1979, whilst the last MR.1 was flown into Woodford for conversion from St.Mawgan on 31st May 1984. While the MR.2 upgrade programme of existing airframes was in progress the eight aircraft in the second production batch (XZ280 – XZ287) was under construction having been ordered as MR.1s. XZ284 however, was completed as an MR.2, the only MR.2 to be completed as such from new. During the 2003 Gulf war a small number of MR.2s received a war fit which included a Forward Looking Infra-Red (FLIR) turret and a Tornado GR.1 type BOZ-107 flare dispenser. Also fitted as an extra self defence measure was an additional underwing BOZ-107 pod containing a Towed Radar Decoy (TRD) system also obtained from the RAF's Tornado force. This pod trailed a wire aerial behind the aircraft terminating in a repeater cone which emitted a false signal to defeat radar guided missiles. The latest obvious external change to the MR.2 concerns its camouflage with a number of aircraft surrendering their NATO Hemp scheme for an even lower visibility two tone grey colour scheme matching current tactical requirements. Nimrods do not carry individual squadron markings though, as all of the aircraft of the

Opposite top: Recovered from the Falklands in 1970 following her abandonment there in 1886, Brunel's SS Great Britain is overflown by MR.1 XV230 whilst being towed to Bristol for long term restoration. Strictly speaking she had not been a steam ship (S.S.) since 1882 when her engines had been removed and the vessel reverted to sail power only. via Andy Evans

Opposite bottom: MR.2 XV229 was an early MR.2 conversion, as yet to receive the later NATO Hemp and Light Aircraft Grey scheme. via Andy Evans

current (in 2006) squadrons are 'pooled' within the Kinloss Wing.

The Nimrod MR.2 carries out three main roles in UK service; anti-submarine warfare, anti-surface unit warfare and search and rescue. Although capable of carrying 25 people, the normal crew complement comprises 13: two pilots and a flight engineer on the flight deck, two navigators, who swap between routine and tactical responsibilities every other sortie, an air electronics officer (AEO), who is both sensor and communications coordinator. The sensor team includes three AEOs (known as 'wet men') who are responsible for monitoring both active (searching) and passive (listening) sonobuoys and four AEOs (known as 'dry men') manage a wide range of avionics and weapon systems essential in delivering Nimrod's capability.

For the Nimrod to perform its tasks the equipment carried is, by its very nature a comprehensive surface and sub-surface search apparatus. Navigation in both the MR.1 and MR.2 is provided by a Decca Doppler operating in conjunction with a Marconi Elliott E3 inertial platform backed by duplicated Sperry GN 7 gyro compasses and an Air Data Computer. A Ferranti FIN 1012 Inertial Navigation System is incorporated in the Nimrod MR.2 to provide improved system performance and reliability and a central computer (a Marconi 920B in the MR.1 and a Marconi 920 ATC in the MR.2) continually calculates the aircraft's present position which is displayed on the Navigator's TV tab display. Other navigation aids available include ADF compasses, VOR/ILS, TACAN and LORAN, with the LORAN being replaced by Omega on the MR.2, which also employs GPS. The automatic flight control system consists of a three-axis Smiths SEP 6 autopilot and an SFS 6 flight system, both integrated with the total navigation kit and twin radio altimeters provide outputs that are fed into the automatic system. Other communications equipment includes the essential personal locater beacon homing set for search and rescue purposes, a secure voice 'scrambler' and an IFF (Identification Friend or Foe) transponder system which could be used in both civil and military modes. The Central Tactical System is the heart of the whole Nimrod weapons ensemble. The information from the navigation system and the tactical sensors is processed by the CTS and displayed on a 24in diameter display screen.

The Nimrod's 'ears' comprise approximately 150 air launched sonobuoys of several different varieties that can be roughly divided into those which listen using the hydrophone principle (passive), and those which emit their own signals and then receive any echoes on the SONAR principle (active). They can be further sub-divided into directional and non-directional variants. Many have become smaller, lighter and cheaper, while others have become larger, more complex and more expensive. Generally the sonobuoys used by Nimrods and by any other type of fixed wing anti-submarine aircraft have to be expendable.

A typical sonobuoy load in a Nimrod could include a selection of the following types.

'Jezebel': Well-proven 'A' size, 3ft long, omni-directional passive buoy which has been used in its thousands for years by the RAF and the Royal Navy.

'Miniature Jezebel': 'F' size (Type SSQ 904) which performs the same functions but is one third the length and about half the weight.

'DIFAR' (Digital Frequency Analysis and Recording): Type AN/SSQ-53; passive, but directional buoy.

'BARRA': Australian-designed directional passive buoy with a high degree of accuracy derived from its five 'arms', each of them carrying five miniature hydrophones, all of which deploy at the preset depth.

Ranger: An omni-directional active buoy based on an American design.

'CAMBS': an abbreviation of Command Active Multibeam Sonobuoy, adjustable by radio command from the air, thus giving it much of the flexibility of the dunking sonar attached by cable to helicopters. Size 'A' and 'F' sonobuoys are launched from the rear fuselage of Nimrod by gravity drop from two six-barrel and two single-barrel launchers.

The Nimrod MR.2's offensive capability is provided by an array of weaponry, and although the original Nimrod pannier was designed to house a mixture of weapons including torpedoes, conventional depth charges and mines, it is the torpedo that has emerged as the prime anti-submarine weapon, whilst the air launched 'over the horizon' AGM-84A Harpoon, has also been adopted in more recent years as an excellent air-to-surface weapon. During the Falklands conflict the Nimrod was also cleared to carry BL755 cluster bombs and wing mounted AIM-9G Sidewinder missiles, the latter capability being retained to attack opposing surveillance aircraft rather than for self-defence alone. It is interesting to record that 1000lb 'iron' bombs were hastily loaded for the Falklands war – but only dropped on training exercises. Originally in the MR.1 and to a lesser extent in the MR.2 both Mk.44 and Mk.46 homing torpedoes would be carried, the MR.2s subsequently being issued with the more advanced Marconi Stingray homing torpedo at the time of the Falklands War. The now obsolete Mk.44 was a 'light-weight' torpedo, electrically propelled, weighing about 233kg, whilst the Mk 46 is a deep-diving, high-speed weapon fitted with an active/passive acoustic homing system specifically intended for use against submarines, and can search for, acquire and then attack, its target. The Stingray includes an on-board computer to control the homing system, sophisticated target detectors and the capability to defeat countermeasures. Provision was made in the earliest Nimrods for underwing pylon-mounted Martel or AS12s air-to-surface missiles but this never came to fruition, although prototype XV148 did test fire 18 of the earlier AS11 missile as well as several AS12 in a series of trials at ranges that varied up to a maximum of five miles. By July 25th 2002 all of the

Nimrod MR.2s had been fitted with the new AQS971 acoustic processor, which replaced the ageing AQS901 unit. Each Nimrod MR.2 has the ability to control 32 sonobouys simultaneously, twice the previous number.

The first loss of a Nimrod occurred on 17th November 1980, when XV256 crashed in the Roseisle Forest after suffering a bird strike on take-off from RAF Kinloss. The captain, Flight Lieutenant Noel Anthony RAAF, and co-pilot, Flying Officer Steve Belcher, were killed although the other 18 on board survived. Another Nimrod was lost on 2nd September 1995 when MR.2 XV239 crashed into Lake Ontario during the Toronto Airshow. All seven crew on board were killed. They were Flight Lieutenant Dom Gilbert (pilot), Flight Lieutenant Glenn Hooper (co-pilot), Flight Lieutenant Bernie Worthington (air electronics officer), Flight Lieutenant Nick Brooks (navigator), Sergeant Gary Moxham (air engineer), and Sergeants Richie Williams and Craig Barnett (air electronics operators). The RAF Board of Inquiry, which reported in November 1996, blamed the crash on pilot error. It concluded that Flight Lieutenant Gilbert had made an 'error of judgement' by tightening one of the turns in the display, and by reducing engine power during the climb immediately preceding it. This reduced the speed of the aircraft to such an extent that safety margins were removed, and the aircraft stalled.

At their peak the Nimrods were located at RAF St.Mawgan in Cornwall, RAF Kinloss in Scotland and Luqa in Malta. No.203 Squadron stationed at Luqa disbanded in 1977 as previously recorded. St.Mawgan hosted No. 42 and No.236 OCU the Nimrod training unit, but during the post Gulf War defence cuts of 1992 the Nimrods were centralised at RAF Kinloss in Scotland, thus ending St.Mawgan's long association with fixed wing aircraft. No.236 OCU was subsequently disbanded, its role being taken by No.42 Squadron which was redesignated No.42 (Reserve) Squadron, the Nimrod OCU. Four Nimrods were withdrawn and placed in storage on 1st October 1992, reducing the force to 26 aircraft. RAF Kinloss on the Moray Firth continues as the operating centre for the MR.2 and the long awaited MRA.4 force, and originally hosted No.120, 201 and 206 Squadrons. As a result of UK defence cuts announced on 21st July 2004, it was decided that the Nimrod MR.2 fleet would be reduced to just 16 aircraft, justified on the basis that the submarine threat has been significantly reduced. The aircraft have now been given a wider tasking remit, undertaking general surveillance duties, latterly during operations over Iraq and Afghanistan. Under further rationalisation No. 206 Squadron was disbanded on 1st April 2005. The last sortie of a 206 crewed Nimrod landed at 11:00 local time at RAF Kinloss on 31st March 2005, flown by pilot Squadron Leader John Leighton, co-pilot Flight Lieutenant Taff Ackland and Air Engineer Squadron Leader John Nelson.

There is always a Nimrod at RAF Kinloss on an hours readiness for search and rescue duties, primarily for downed military aircrew and military maritime incidents. Nimrods are tasked by the Air Rescue Coordination Centre, co-located at Kinloss, to attend many civil incidents, and such activities may include carrying out searches, assisting search and rescue helicopters or acting as on-scene commander during major incidents such as the Piper Alpha oil-rig disaster for instance.

MR.2 XV232 of No.206 Squadron. via Andy Evans

Right: *MR.2P XV227. Shown to advantage this photograph reveals the extent of the 'double bubble' effect created by the addition of the ventral pannier.*

Below: *MR.2P XV248. A good view of the ex-Vulcan in-flight refuelling probe fitted above the cabin, as a direct result of the Falklands War of 1982. In the early days aircrew had to get used to the fuel line running along the cabin floor! Note also the 'eyebrow' windows which allow Nimrod pilots an additional measure of visibility during tight turns that may be experienced in ASW flying. The 'eyebrows' did not feature on the Comet or the two Nimrod prototypes.*
Both Mathew Clements

Above: *XV241 on the 16th October 1994 in the 80th Anniversary colours of No.206 Squadron.* via Andy Evans

Left: *An unidentified Nimrod undergoing extensive servicing at Kinloss. The Searchwater radar scanner and the fixing points for the in-flight refuelling probe are shown to advantage.* Matthew Clements

Above: *MR.2P XV233 stands adorned with its No.42 Squadron anniversary tail markings. See colour side view.* Gordon Bartley

Right: *MR.2P XV241 of 120 Squadron escorting B-24 Liberator* Diamond Lil *on 3rd June 1992. 'Lil' was originally destined for 120 Squadron during WW2 but a pre-delivery accident prevented her from doing so.* via Andy Evans

Opposite top: *MR.2P XV255 on patrol, paying attention to the trawler below.* BAe Systems

Opposite bottom: *MR.2P XV241 literally on coastal patrol in Scotland.* BAe Systems

Top: *MR.2P XV232 on patrol with a sister Nimrod, whose 70 million candle power Strong Electric searchlight can be seen on the extreme right of this photograph. XV232 is carrying a BOZ-107 chaff and flare dispenser.*
Gordon Bartley

Above: *MR.2P XV241 on coastal patrol again displaying the BOZ-107 pod borrowed from the Tornado GR.1 force.*
BAe Systems

Top: *MR.2P XV238 landing at Lossiemouth, Scotland, in June 1991.*

Above: *MR.2P XV234 in July 1992. Note the patch painting on various panels along the fuselage and the larger area of patch painting around the cockpit and nose.* Both Terry Senior

Above: *This pair of submarines are no doubt fully aware of the Nimrods ability to hunt and kill them were they hostile. BAe Systems*

Right: *Close up detail of a FLIR turret and BOZ pod. Tim Senior*

Opposite top and bottom: *During the 2003 Gulf War a small number of MR.2Ps received a war fit which included a FLIR turret, a Tornado-based BOZ-107 flare dispenser, and underwing Towed Radar Decoy pod installed as additional self defence measures in the earlier 1992 conflict. BAe Systems*

MR.2P XV246 above on 26th May 2001 and XV236 below, date unknown. Clearly seen on each wing tip are the avionics tactical sensor pods known as 'Yellowgate' electronic support measures (ESM). These passive electronic modules were originally designed as radar warning receivers (RWR) for the AEW.3 and reprogrammed as ESM to listen to and classify electronic emissions emanating from hostile territory, these are then displayed on one of the work stations. On top of the tail is the 'inverted football' fairing containing further passive ESM antennae, each able to detect signals on differing wave bands. Similar equipment is fitted on the R.1s and will be fitted to the MRA.4.
Terry Senior top, Andy Evans below

Above: MR.2P XV236. The latest and most obvious external change to the MR.2 is to their camouflage, with a number of aircraft surrendering their NATO Hemp for an even lower visibility two tone grey colour scheme, comprising in this instance Camouflage Grey with Light Aircraft Grey undersurfaces.

Below: R.1s have also had the new colours applied but in a different fashion and this unidentified R.1 has Light Aircraft Grey above the cockpit extending to base of the tail. The remainder of the aircraft is Camouflage Grey. Both Gordon Bartley

Chapter 2: ELECTRONIC INTELLIGENCE, AIRBORNE EARLY WARNING AND THE MRA.4

BAe Nimrod R Mk 1

Below: *Comet R.2 XK659 seen at Luqa Malta on 14th December 1966, whilst serving with 51 Squadron with which unit she remained until struck off charge on 13th May 1974. 51 Squadron operated three R.2s, the others being XK665 and XK663, the latter being damaged beyond repair in a hanger fire at Watton on 3rd June 1959. XK663 was later replaced by XK695, a C.2 which following conversion was redesignated R.2.*
Newark Air Museum

The most secretive of all the Nimrod versions are the trio of Electronic Intelligence (ELINT) gathering R.1s operated by No.51 Squadron at RAF Waddington. These aircraft undertake their role in the shadows, and their operations rarely come into the public gaze. When No.192 Squadron was re-numbered 51 Squadron on 21st August 1958, the unit operated as a Special Duties squadron in Signals Command, flying Comets and a variety of Canberras on surveillance flights from RAF Wyton. Immediate attention was turned to identifying a replacement for the three venerable Comet R.2s which would approach the end of their useful lives by the early 1970s. Air Staff Requirement 389 was issued detailing the characteristics required for a SIGINT aircraft to replace the Comets. It was quickly apparent that the flexibility required for

major differences notably the lack of a Magnetic Anomaly Detector (MAD) boom, a number of cabin windows blocked to allow installation of more equipment, dieletric radomes in the nose of each external wing tank and also in the tailcone, with copious quantities of aerials and antennae referred to as the 'farm'. Internally, the aircraft are completely different, apart from the flight deck area. Because of the sensitivity of the equipment involved, the aircraft were delivered essentially as 'empty shells' to RAF Wyton where they were fitted out with their electronic 'wizardry'. The flight deck area consists of five crew (two pilots, two navigators and a flight engineer) but additional space is available for two supplementary flight crew to provide relief on long sorties. Accurate navigation is essential and the aircraft are fitted with an AD360 ADF, AD260 VOR/ILS, AN/ARN-172 TACAN, AN/ARA-50 UFH DF, LORAN, and a Kollsman periscope sextant. The ASV-21D radar from the ASW Nimrod was retained with its 32 inch diameter dish. Up to 23 SIGINT specialists are accommodated at 13 side facing equipment consoles in the fuselage; consoles 1-5 are located on the port side with consoles 6-13 on the starboard side. Each console is designed to accommodate two four foot modules with provision for a single seat placed centrally but able to slide on transverse rails. Consoles 1-4 and 9-12 also have provision for a pair of side by side seats, and additionally three forward facing single consoles now augment these double consoles.

Opposite page:

Top: *Nimrod R.1 XW665 in original livery at Wyton in June 1980. Note the 51 Squadron motif which represents a goose, their motto being: Swift and Sure.*

Centre: *R.1 XW664 at an unknown location in September 1991.*

Bottom: *R.1 XW664 at Waddington on 22nd June 1995. By this time the national markings had been reduced in size and in this photograph and the one above the squadron motif has been rendered differently from XW665.*
All Terry Senior

ASW operations made the Nimrod ideal for gathering electronic intelligence and procurement staff soon focused on the HS 801 Nimrod Anti-Submarine Warfare (ASW) aircraft already being purchased for the RAF. On operational sorties the Comet R.2 often operated in conjunction with a No.51 Squadron Canberra, however, the endurance and equipment aboard the Nimrod soon allowed the latter aircraft to operate without additional support. In 1969 three Nimrods were ordered for No.51 Squadron, initially as HS 801Rs, but later changed to Nimrod R.1s. The cost of developing the three specially configured aircraft was estimated at £2.38m with production costing £11.34m. Additional special equipment accounted for £1.25m and additional COMINT equipment such as magnetic tape recorders, TR1986/1987 and R216 receiver replacements, and an aerial distribution system and auto voice indicator added another estimated £545,000.

Although externally the airframe of the Nimrod R.1 is essentially the same as the Nimrod MR.1, there are

The first Nimrod R.1, XW664, was delivered to RAF Wyton on 7th July 1971 and took over two years to fit out. The first training sortie captained by Flight Lieutenant Gordon Lambert was flown on 21st October 1973 with the first operational sortie being flown on 3rd May 1974 with the type being formally commissioned into RAF service on 10th May 1974. Two more Nimrod R.1s, XW665 and XW666, entered service during late 1974, thus allowing the retirement of the last Comets and Canberras. No.51 Squadron also received a standard Nimrod MR.1 XZ283 on 8th April 1976, staying with the squadron probably in an aircrew training role, until June 1978 when it was returned to BAe for conversion to AEW.3 standard. Another Nimrod MR.1 XV252 then briefly acted as the trainer until the squadron reverted to the three operational aircraft.

In 1980 the aircraft were upgraded by replacing the ASV21 ASW radar with an ECKO 290 weather radar display in the cockpit, this allowed the radar navigator crew position to be removed. The workload of the single navigator was improved by removing one of the LORAN sets and replacing it with a Delco AN/ASN-119

Top: *R.1 XW665 at Wyton in July 1987.* Terry Senior

Above: *R.1 XW664 at Waddington in 1995.* via Andy Evans

Right: *R.1 XW665 at Waddington on 2nd July 2001, by which date the goose has altered in form once again.* Tim Senior

Carrousel IVA INS. As a result of this upgrade one of the external LORAN aerials was removed and a variety of other external antennae appeared, believed to be used for direction finding. Wingtip pods, similar in appearance to the Yellow Gate Electronic Support Measures (ESM) fitted to the Nimrod MR.2 also appeared on XW664 and these were later added to the other two aircraft. The requirement for in-flight refuelling became apparent as a result of the Falkland's War, however, the probes were not actually fitted until after the conflict was over. Along with the refuelling probe each aircraft also gained a large ventral fin, overwing vortex generators and rectangular tailplane finlets. Underwing pylons were also fitted at the same time and these now carry a modified BOZ pod containing a GEC-Marconi towed radar decoy system similar to that used by the RAF's Tornado force. A further upgrade saw the aircraft being outfitted with a Marconi Master satellite communications system.

Nimrod R.1 XW666 was jokingly referred to by some personnel on No.51 Squadron as 'The Beast' or 'Damian', because of the 'satanic' connotations of the number 666. Unfortunately, this came back to haunt them when on 16th May 1995, during an air-test, following a lengthy stay at the Nimrod Major Servicing Unit at Kinloss, a starter motor blew itself to pieces and the debris punctured the aircraft's wing and fuel tanks. A catastrophic fire broke out which was so severe that there was every likelihood the main spar holding the wing onto the fuselage would burn through and fail. The pilot of the aircraft, Flight Lieutenant Art Stacey, had no choice but to carry out an immediate ditching in the Moray Firth from which all the crew survived. Flight Lieutenant Stacey was subsequently awarded the Air Force Cross. Fortunately conditions for ditching were ideal, and all seven crew members were able to get into dinghies before being picked up by a Sea King HC.3 from Lossiemouth. The wreckage was subsequently recovered from 70ft of water and was later scrapped, although the remains of the front fuselage exists at Aeroventure, Doncaster. Nimrod MR.2, XV249 (held in storage), was identified as a suitable replacement and after a major overhaul at RAF Kinloss the aircraft was ferried to BAe Woodford and stripped of all ASW equipment. After the installation of some antenna fairings, the aircraft was ferried to RAF Waddington on 19th December 1996.

During the mid-1990's the Nimrods were again on the receiving end of some modifications under the aegis of Project 'Starwindow'. This project had been launched to equip the R.1s with a new Open Systems architecture digital SIGINT suite, probably based on that carried by the RC-135 Rivet Joint aircraft operated by the USAF. The 'Starwindow' system incorporates two high-speed search receivers, a wide band digital direction finding system and 22 pooled digital intercept receivers. New workstations were fitted for the 'specialists' in the rear of the aircraft. The 'Starwindow' installation on XV249 (the XW666 replacement),

began on 27th December 1996 and the aircraft eventually flew as a fully equipped R.1 on 11th April 1997. In addition to the Starwindow package the R.1s were also fitted with a new 'Special Signals' intercept facility with a digital recording and playback suite, an enhanced pulse-signal processing capability and multi channel digital data demodulator. With the R.1s scheduled to remain in service until at least 2012 a further equipment improvement programme known as 'Extract', completed a mission system upgrade on the three aircraft in 2003. Project 'Extract' replaced manual collection systems with automated collection equipment, and added other hardware and software enhancements. A further programme currently under consideration and seemingly set to be awarded in 2007, is Project 'HELIX'. This is aimed at maintaining the effectiveness of the Nimrod R.1 fleet up to 2025, and includes upgrades to the aircraft mission systems, associated ground stations and training facilities. Currently there is no planned replacement for the R.1. The Nimrod R.1s have also been repainted in a low visibility Light Aircraft Grey and Camouflage Grey scheme replacing the former Hemp and Light Aircraft Grey colours.

During the conflicts that have occurred over the last three decades, the Nimrod R.1s have quietly plied their trade operating in the background of the wars. During the Falklands War ('Operation Corporate') in 1982 it is believed that R.1 XW664, operated from a base in Chile alongside a detachment of RAF Canberra PR9s, but this remains unconfirmed. In August 1990 when Iraq invaded and occupied Kuwait, the British response, 'Operation Granby', commenced immediately and No.51 Squadron was deployed to the area and remained in theatre until March 1991 in support of operations 'Desert Shield' and 'Desert Storm' and was later involved in 'Operation Bolton' during mid-1998, culminating in providing invaluable support to allied aircraft participating in 'Operation Desert Fox' during the December of that year. The squadron then returned to normal duties until June 1991 when it was tasked to fly operations in the Adriatic, which it continues to do to this day. In June 1992, the squadron commenced regular deployments to Italy and carried out operations in support of United Nations (UN) operations in the Former Republic of Yugoslavia (FYR), and once the UN mandate ended No.51 Squadron continued to support IFOR and SFOR (the NATO implementation and stabilisation forces in the FYR.). During the more recent 'Iraqi Freedom' campaign of 2003 the R.1s were again called into action. The unit's long association with RAF Wyton was brought to an end in 1995 when the trio of R.1s moved to the RAF specialist surveillance base at RAF Waddington to join the E-3 Sentry force and the new Sentinel R.1 ASTOR aircraft of No.5 Squadron, which accepted its first aircraft as recently as June 2007.

Opposite top and centre: MR.2 XV249, previously held in storage, was considered to be a suitable replacement for XW666 and was flown to BAe Woodford for partial conversion to R.1 standard following the removal of anti-submarine warfare equipment. On 19th December 1996 XV249 was flown to RAF Waddington for the conversion to be completed. Seen on 21st March 1997 at Waddington, two views of XV249 in an interim state. The external modifications and paint condition are self evident. Terry Senior

Opposite bottom: R.1 XV249 at RAF Waddington on 5th July 1999. All Terry Senior

R.1 XW666 'Damien' or 'The Beast' at Wyton in May 1979. Terry Senior

No.51 Squadron

Motto - Swift and Sure.
Badge - A goose volant - approved by King George VI in December 1937. It was chosen as a play on the word 'Anson', which the Squadron was flying when the badge was being designed, as 'Anser' is the Latin word for Goose, and it was felt that a heavy wild fowl was appropriate for a bomber squadron.

No.51 Squadron formed at Thetford, Norfolk, on 15th May 1916 as a Home Defence unit equipped with Royal Aircraft Factory B.E.2 and B.E.12 aircraft. For the remainder of the First World War, the squadron flew its B.E.2s and B.E.12s on anti-Zeppelin patrols, the unit also providing night flying training for newly qualified pilots with Avro 504Ks. In June 1919, the Squadron was disbanded at Sutton's Farm, Hornchurch. The squadron reformed on 5th March 1937 when 'B' Flight of No 58 Squadron, was renumbered at Driffield. Vickers Virginias and Avro Ansons were flown until Armstong Whitworth Whitleys arrived in early 1938, and it was with these aircraft that the squadron flew its first operational missions of the Second World War. The flights took place on the very first night of the War, 3rd/4th September 1939, and the squadron dropped leaflets over Germany. Bombing missions started in May 1940, and continued until 1942 when No.51 was assigned to anti-submarine patrols over the Bay of Biscay as part of Coastal Command. The following year, the Handley Page Halifax replaced the ageing Whitleys and the unit returned to Bomber Command as a 'main force' squadron for the remainder of the European War. Within weeks of the wars end, the Squadron had transferred to Transport Command converting to Short Stirlings for troop and freight flights to India. These aircraft were in turn replaced during 1946 with Avro Yorks. In August 1948, the unit transferred to Wunsdorf in Germany and joined 'Operation Plainfare', the Berlin Airlift, flying supplies into the German capital. A year later, No.51 relocated to Bassingbourn and took up long-range route flying until it was disbanded in October 1950. The Squadron reformed in August 1958 when No.192 Squadron based at Watton was redesignated. The unit operated as a Special Duties squadron in Signals Command flying Comets and Canberras on surveillance flights from Wyton until 1974 when the Comets were replaced by the specialised Nimrod R.1, now based at Waddington, as part of No.2 Group.

The 'Beast's' demise. R.1 XW666 following ditching in the Moray Firth, North Sea on 16th May 1995 whilst carrying out an air test. via Gordon Bartley

Nimrod AEW.3

The ability to see 'over the horizon' and detect at an early stage aircraft and missiles being deployed in anger is vital. The Airborne Early Warning (AEW) aircraft was therefore seen as a vital link in the defence chain, and for the RAF the choice of its new 'aerial eyes' to replace its veteran Shackleton AEW aircraft was at best short sighted, and at worst a total disaster. The debacle that was the Nimrod AEW.3 programme will stand out as possibly one of the great British defence procurement fiascos of all time. It was certainly one of the most expensive and the final bill to the UK taxpayer has probably never been accurately calculated, but even the most conservative estimate of £1 billion takes little account of the damage caused to the reputations of the companies involved.

With the advent of the Falklands War in 1982, the eventual success of the Task Force was based on a little luck, the Sea Harrier, and the British 'make do' spirit. The defence review of 1965 had begun the process of ending the era of the Royal Navy's large aircraft carriers, each capable of operating a flight of fixed-wing Airborne Early Warning aircraft, the Fairey Gannet AEW.3. Consequently, by 1982 the RN lacked any organic AEW capability to send with the Falklands Task Force, a role that in theory should have been provided by the RAF with the Nimrod AEW.3, but at that time the programme was in a state of almost total shambles. The overall result was the loss of a number of ships to air attack and the deaths of many whose lives might well have been saved if an AEW aircraft had been available. Just how this might have been achieved though, when it required virtually the whole of the UK's air-to-air resources to get one Vulcan there and back is a debate for another day!

When Grumman and General Electric began development of the E-2 Hawkeye in the early 1960s, the capability of this carrier based AEW radar, operating at UHF wavelengths with an Airborne Moving Target Indicator (ATMI), was set to revolutionise AEW development. British industry and the Ministry of Defence watched the development in the USA with some consternation, realising that unless they set about finding a replacement for the antiquated Gannet, they would be out of the AEW market forever. Various design ideas were considered, including a Blackburn Buccaneer with two sideways facing antennas in the bombbay and a Hawker Siddeley HS.125 (later adopted as the RAF's Dominie T.1 navigation trainer) with a mushroom radome mounted above the fuselage – however, this is where the problems began. The E-2 Hawkeye is a very clever design, which compresses two flight crew, three systems operators and a considerable amount of electronic equipment into an airframe small enough to operate from a carrier whilst carrying a rotordome – an achievement no other country has been able to match. Size became a crucial factor in the British design proposals when it was decided

that a rotordome mounted radar which met the design specification, could not be carried on an HS.125-sized aircraft and attention switched to a new design with a Fore and Aft Scanner System (FASS).

By 1965 British industry was keen to develop Frequency-Modulated Intermittent Continuous-Wave (FMICW) radar using elliptical or circular inverted-cassegrain antennas. The properties of these types of radar did not allow them to operate effectively near propellers, so the proposed AEW aircraft had to be jet powered. Again size became a factor and it was soon apparent that the large antennas necessary to meet the range criteria, together the associated equipment and crew, could only be carried by a fairly large aircraft - certainly one much too big to fit on an aircraft carrier, which was lucky for them, as the Labour government of the day had by then decided to get rid of them! Various options were considered for a FASS installation including a jet-powered version of the HS.748 Andover and the BAC 1-11, before engineers finally settled on an adaptation of the proposed HS.801 anti-submarine version of the Comet – the Nimrod.

Eventually UK scientists deciding to drop the FMICW radar in favour of a pulse-Doppler set and

funding for the system was finally approved in 1972. Various options for the Nimrod airframe were considered; the initial idea involved mounting the E-2C AN/APS-125 radar and associated avionics above and inside the airframe. The second option was to use the AN/APS-125 radar with British avionics. The third option was to mount the AN/APA-171 radome and antenna on the Nimrod, with Britain supplying the radar transmitter, receiver and avionics. The fourth option was an all British radar and avionics system, with some American components, and a FASS with pulse-Doppler processing operating in the S-band. Although this fourth option provided the greatest input from British industry, it also carried the greatest technical risk but the political considerations in keeping BAe & GEC workers employed outweighed common sense. By the end of 1974, instead of purchasing an off the shelf system with a proven track record, as was

Opposite top: R.1 XW665 in level flight with an unidentified R.1 banking away in 2004. Neatly indicated is the manner in which Hemp wrapped around the leading edges of the wings and the demarcation between Hemp and Light Aircraft Grey on the ventral fuselage.

Opposite bottom: R.1 XW665 in 2006 believed to be landing at RAF Waddington and by now displaying the current Camouflage Grey scheme with Light Aircraft Grey fuselage top.
Both via Andy Evans

Above: A close up of the bulbous nose of trials Comet 4C XW626 (ex G-APDS). Less streamlined than that of the AEW3, but adequate to prove the concept.
Gordon Bartley

Top: *XW626 ex Comet 4C G-APDS resplendent in its red white and grey colour scheme shows its bulbous nose for the Fore and Aft Scanner System (FASS) trials. Note the 'AEW Radar Trials' logo visible on the fuselage side and the Nimrod style fin fitted to compensate for the radome.*

Above: *XW626 showing lots of detail. Of note are the red wing panels and the thin stripes along the wing tanks and the instrument probe protruding from the starboard tank.*

Right: *This view of AEW3 XZ286 (DB1) shows its twin hemisphere radomes to good effect.* All Terry Senior

the Boeing E-3A AWACS, the Labour government decided to press ahead with the Nimrod AEW.3, accepting whatever extra cost and technical risk that was inevitably involved. Interestingly though, the Labour government of the day had strangely decided that joining a possible NATO purchase of the Boeing E-3A was just too politically complicated, expensive and subject to unknown delay!

To facilitate proving the concept of the FASS, a modified Comet 4C XW626 fitted with a forward scanner was used for a series of trials to prove the basic concept of the system. Following these trials, on 31st March 1977, the Government gave the go ahead for Hawker Siddeley to supply the airframe and Marconi-Elliot, (later Marconi Avionics) to supply the Mission System Avionics (MSA) and, between them, convert and deliver 11 Nimrod AEW.3 aircraft. These airframes comprised of eight already built and in storage and a further three that became available when No.203 Squadron disbanded following the RAF withdrawal from Malta. The principal airframe design changes from the maritime Nimrods to the AEW.3s were instantly obvious. Most striking were the large bulbous radomes mounted fore and aft, that were to house the 180° radar scanners and the addition of new wing tip mounted Yellowgate ESM pods, developed from an earlier RWR design and only just beginning to appear on Nimrod MR.2s. Under the fore-and-aft radar arrangement each radar antenna made a 180° active sweep followed by a 'dead' return. The movements were synchronised to provide the overall 360° cover needed. The antennae were some eight feet wide and six feet high and stabilised in pitch and roll by gyro platforms with computer processing being used to handle returns from all the sensors to provide the automatic tracking of targets. The internal fit contained three main sensors to detect, track and classify targets, these being the radar, passive radio and radar detection systems (ESM), and an IFF to identify friendly forces. The radar would pass the target information in terms of range azimuth, velocity and height to the data handling system; this was collated via the ESM and IFF. The pulse Doppler system worked well during over water operations, and was advertised as having sophisticated anti-jamming devices.

The radomes, designed by Marconi, contrasted markedly with the Boeing AWACS configuration. It was originally hoped that the AEW.3 radomes would each be of the same size and shape as each other, but the nose unit had to be profiled sharply to cope with bird strike and rain erosion as well as presenting a clean aerodynamic flow. Installing the same shape on the tail would have led to an unstable airflow so a more rounded configuration had to be adopted. The positioning of both radomes was also governed to some extent by ground clearance. Surprisingly these large additions to the nose and tail of the aircraft had a beneficial, rather than detrimental effect on directional stability. This was partly because the thicker rear fuse-lage shape added to the total keel area aft effectively increasing the original fin area. As weapons were not carried, the pannier space could be used for fuel, thereby giving the aircraft a total endurance well above the MR.2s normal 12 hours on internal fuel alone.

The 1976 operating specification of the planned Nimrod AEW.3, ASR 400, was proving to be very demanding. It called for exceptional detection capabilities of vessels at sea and aircraft over land and sea, far in excess of the E-2C and with the ability to automatically initiate and track up to 400 targets. Six operator's consoles (four radar, one communications and one for ESM) were planned and, although double the number of the E-2C, it was much less than the nine originally planned for the E-3A, which also featured considerable empty space for additional consoles should the need arise. The Nimrod AEW.3 was further required to carry a comprehensive communications fit, which would allow combined operations with NATO E-3As. However, space was always at a premium, as the Nimrod AEW.3 was planned to be about half the weight of an E-3A, (but three times that of the E-2C) and a sheer lack of space eventually became one of the major problems bedevilling this project. In 1977 ASR 400 was re-drafted to ASR 400 Revision 1, however, it was never clearly established as to which standard the production aircraft were to be produced becoming another classic example of lack of communication between contractor and the customer.

Despite the chaotic project management of the earlier TSR-2, which contributed considerably to its eventual cancellation, similar problems began to occur in the project management of the Nimrod AEW.3. The normal procedure for a project of this size was for the RAF Operational Requirements (OR) branch to lead the project through the feasibility stage, with the operational aspects stated by the Assistant Chief of the Air Staff (ACAS) and financial input from the Air Plans branch. The Ministry of Defence (Procurement Executive) Controller of Aircraft (MOD[PE] CA) had responsibility for project definition and development, usually under an assistant director. Reporting to the MOD(PE) CA was the Director of Military Aircraft Projects, who had a Nimrod director and an assistant Nimrod director, and it was this individual who was actually responsible for the AEW.3. Generally, the individual in this appointment was a Wing Commander, a rank too junior to carry any real influence with the MOD. However, responsibility for the electronic systems in the AEW.3 lay elsewhere, namely with the Director of Air Weapons and Electronic Systems, whose Assistant Director Electronics, Radar (Airborne) was actually responsible for this vital equipment. Ultimate financial authority rested with the Minister of State for Defence, and although representatives of the various parties with a vested interest in the project should have met 'as necessary', this proved to occur only at the quarterly review boards. Essentially, the prime contractors were left to sort out the physical integration of the various systems, with minimal input from the MOD or RAF.

As stated earlier a total of 11 AEW.3 aircraft were to be produced. Three, XZ286, XZ287 and XZ281, were to be used as development aircraft, supported by comprehensive test rig installations at both Marconi and BAe (previously Hawker Siddeley) at Woodford. These three aircraft were later refurbished to full production standard. The remainder were to be built as production aircraft for delivery to the RAF. On 16th July 1980, trials airframe XZ286 made its first flight from Woodford flown by Charles Masefield, BAe Manchester's Chief Test Pilot and was airborne for three and a half hours. This aircraft was not equipped with Mission System Avionics (MSA) and was used for airframe performance and handling trials, as well as development of the engineering systems required to support the MSA. It was later joined on flight trials by XZ287 in January 1981 and XZ281 in July 1981, both of these aircraft being allocated for the development and clearance of the Marconi MSA.

In late 1984 The first production AEW.3 XZ285 was transferred from Woodford to its proposed new home at Waddington, becoming the first airframe for the new Joint Trials Unit, (JTU) it still being unclear at this point whether the Nimrod AEW force would become No.8 Squadron replacing the existing Shackleton AEW aircraft. At this stage the AEW Nimrods were all wearing the familiar MR.1 grey and white colour schemes with tan fore and aft radomes.

The Joint Trials Unit was established to help develop the Mission System Avionics (MSA) and in no time at all serious problems with the MSA were identified. The heart of the MSA was the GEC 4080M computer that received data from the previously noted radar scanners, the Loral ARI-18240/1 ESM system, the Cossor Jubilee Guardsman IFF equipment and the two Ferranti FIN 1012 inertial navigation systems. The computer processed this mass of data and then displayed it on the multi function display and control consoles (MDCC) where the operators communicated to the various command organisations and operational units through the Automatic Management of Radio and Intercom Systems (AMRICS). Independently, these systems worked correctly, but after they were integrated serious problems emerged. The fundamental problem was that the computer simply was not powerful enough. The GEC 4080M computer had a storage capacity of a paltry 1 megabyte which could be augmented via a data-bus with an additional 1.4 megabytes, giving a grand total of just 2.4 megabytes total storage capacity, small even by the standards of the time and particularly so given the task it had to perform: just relate this to your home computer of today! The computer quickly showed it was too slow for the task and soon became overloaded, at which point track continuity suffered, this then led to track duplication, which slowly increased and further overloaded the system. Another major problem was the sheer amount of heat generated by all the electronics when operating the radar and other systems at full power. This was a real problem, because the fuel system was used as a 'heat-sink' and to be able to dissipate the heat generated when the MSA and radar operated at full power, the fuel tanks needed to be at least half full, which was at odds with the Nimrods basic fuel management system.

Essentially, like so many other MOD procurement disasters, the Nimrod AEW.3 suffered from requirements that constantly changed, inadequate project management and, in an attempt to save money, the 'bodged' adaptation of an elderly airframe, rather than affording a new airframe designed exactly for the purpose. Although the Nimrod AEW project struggled on, the MSA could rarely be made to work consistently. Under test by the MOD(PE) in 1984 the MSA, whilst falling short of the ASR 400 requirements, could work well and showed promise, but it was very unreliable and its performance changed from sortie to sortie. During the first eight sorties only three hours of full system operation was achieved. Detection range was 30% below the specified distance, tracking continuity was erratic with numerous false plots, all round surveillance was poor and did not provide the anticipated twin hemispheric coverage and last, but not least, maritime detection resolution was poor. All the time the costs mounted, with little sign that this monstrous white elephant would ever work as required. Finally, common sense prevailed and in 1986 the axe fell, bringing the curtain down on the entire farce which ended by costing the taxpayer somewhere in the region of £1 billion. In 1988 a Boeing proposal for the supply of seven E-3D Sentrys was accepted and this aircraft eventually entered service in 1991. It is worth recapping that during the sad debacle, the airframes ability to carry the installations were never called into question. Other than the initial AEW.3 DB1 (Development Batch) XZ286 the programme also involved aircraft DB2 XZ287, DB3 XZ281 and the first production PI XZ285. DB2 and DB3 were operated from Woodford by BAe and GEC Avionics, frequently carrying MoD(PE) Establishments' specialists, and PI was operated by the Joint Trials Unit (JTU) established at RAF Waddington. Of the remaining aircraft involved in the programme, production aircraft P4 XZ283 was delivered from Woodford to RAF Waddington in November 1985 and P3 XV263 was scheduled to be delivered at the end of that year. At the end of 1985 P5 XZ280 and Development Batch aircraft DB1 XZ286 were being equipped with their MSAs at Woodford. The remaining aircraft P2 XV259, P6 XZ282, P7 XV262 and P8 XV261 were effectively complete and awaiting their outfitting.

The Nimrod AEW airframes all met an ignominious end. Some remained in open storage at RAF Finningley as static ground instructional airframes, whilst others were sent to RAF Abingdon where they were stripped of their useful parts and used as fire training

hulks. Today only the nose section of XW259 remains, at the Solway Aviation Museum. Some photographic evidence exits to suggest that a fuselage existed at Abingdon until 2003. At RAF Waddington some of the infrastructure from the project still exists in No.5 and No.3 hangars, particularly the huge hydraulic servicing rigs with service points built into the hangar floors.

To fill the 'AEW gap' as the AEW Gannets were progressively retired (the last leaving service in 1978) and before the Nimrod AEW.3 was due to enter service in 1981, the RAF was forced to convert 12 obsolete Shackleton MR.2 aircraft to carry the obsolescent AP/APS-20 radar removed from the Gannets. Entering service with No.8 Squadron at RAF Lossiemouth in 1972, the Shackleton was cold, incredibly noisy and thoroughly uncomfortable for the crew – high-tone deafness after a couple of tours was routine. It was often said that one of the nicest sounds in the world was a Shackleton getting airborne, because that meant you weren't on board. Unpressurised, the Shackleton was limited to around 10,000ft and usually operated at a much lower altitude. The APS-20 radar had a range of only 100 miles and had no height finding capability, so in reality there was little point in flying high anyway. However, because of the Nimrod AEW.3 fiasco, five of these obsolete, antiquated, uncomfortable aircraft had to soldier on for 20 years until the Boeing E-3D entered service in 1991!

Opposite top: AEW.3 P4 XZ283 at Waddington in December 1985.

Opposite bottom: AEW.3 P2 XV259 at Waddington in the mid 1980s. Both Terry Senior

This view of P1 XZ285, at Waddington, gives a good impression of just how much work went into the AEW airframe development. Here the aircraft is painted in its primer coat. Chris Muir

AEW.3 P1 XZ285 also at Waddington, date unknown. Terry Senior

Left: *An unusual view of the distinctive forward radome of AEW.3 P1 XZ285 at RAF Finningley in September 1985.* Martin Derry

Below: *Redundant AEW.3 airframes in mid-1989, DB3 XZ281, P4 XZ283 and DB2 XZ287 amongst them. Presumably in storage at RAF Abingdon judging by the presence of ex-civil VC-10s, some later used in the RAF VC-10 tanker fleet programme.* Terry Senior

Bottom: *AEW.3 P3 XV263 relegated as the Air Engineers Squadron ground instructional aircraft at Finningley in September 1991. Note the large Engineer trade artwork behind the cockpit.* Andy Evans Collection

Nimrod MRA.4

By the early 1990s it was becoming apparent that a replacement for the Nimrod would be required, the airframe, engines and avionics were all starting to show their age and the only sensible solution was a new aircraft that could take advantage of significant improvements in engine performance, avionics and onboard equipment. The basic requirement for the new aircraft was agreed and in November of 1992 a study was undertaken to determine what outline type would be needed for the replacement aircraft. At first it appeared likely that the existing MR.2s would be given another upgrade and refurbished, but this would prove to be too expensive, so attention switched to the purchase of a new version of the Lockheed P-3 Orion, to be known as P-7, which the US Navy were also looking to order. Eventually the US Navy decided not to continue with the P-7 programme leaving the RAF to consider other options. Therefore a competitive tendering phase between potential contractors began in January 1995 under Air Staff Requirement 420, thereby giving the RAF the chance to assess all the latest maritime patrol aircraft. Competing for the order were the Dassault Atlantique 3, Lockheed Martin Orion 2000, Loral/Marshall Valkyrie and the proposed BAe Nimrod 2000, a reworked version of the MR.2. The result was announced on 2nd December 1996, and a fixed-price contract worth £2.2bn for 21 Nimrod aircraft, training systems and initial support was signed, and unsurprisingly BAe systems were the company nominated to produce a 'new' aircraft – known at the time as the Nimrod 2000. However, to reduce the overall cost, and in keeping with the Ministry of Defence's desire for a commercial off-the-shelf solution, the BAe proposal relied on using the fuselages from a number of current Nimrod MR.2s, a decision seen by many to be more than a little controversial. The original contract called for 21 fully equipped aircraft, but this figure was later reduced to 18, then in a shock announcement this was cut to just 12 after the Ministry of Defence re-assessed the future threats and the improvements gained by the use of updated equipment. The changing face of global warfare had a marked effect on the RAF's forward planning, and in particular the role of the proposed Nimrod 2000 following the virtual disintegration of the Warsaw Pact and its feared submarine threat which had been a key feature in the original Nimrod concept. During its time in RAF service the Nimrod MR.2 was adapted to fulfil other roles, and with the addition of surveillance cameras on four aircraft a new dimension to the mighty hunter was created. In recognition of these and other new areas of expertise and the prospect of those planned for the replacement aircraft, the Nimrod 2000 was renamed Nimrod Maritime, Reconnaissance and Attack Mk.4 (MRA.4) in early 1998. Given the nature of the current global threats, there is every likelihood that the new aircraft will spend far more time on reconnaissance, ELINT and communication relay duties, than on traditional maritime patrols, their abilities will complement the three continually over-tasked ELINT Nimrod R.1s of No.51 Squadron.

As noted earlier, controversy was firmly in the mix with the decision by BAe in their study to determine the design for the MRA.4, to refurbish and reuse the fuselages of a number of old Nimrods as the baseline for the new aircraft. To some extent this decision was driven by the political desire of the MOD to procure a derivative of an existing aircraft, and therefore saving money. In hindsight, it would probably have been easier to have built completely new fuselages and even though the original jigs were destroyed by BAe many years ago, reopening a complete assembly line would have enabled any number of aircraft to be built and perhaps marketed and sold to other countries. However, the first three fuselages allocated for refurbishment were stripped of all equipment and flown from Kinloss to FRA/Serco at Bournemouth, Hurn, between 14-16th of February 1997, inside an Antonov An-124. FRA/Serco were sub-contracted by BAe to completely re-life the fuselages to give them another 25 years of service, but it soon became obvious that they could not meet the planned timetable within the agreed costs. Eventually, these aircraft were transferred back to BAe at Woodford for the work to be completed, but by the time everything had been sorted out the entire programme had slipped 23 months.

However, to describe the MRA.4 simply as a refurbished MR.2 is to ignore the fact that it is essentially a new aircraft. In fact the only parts of the old MR.2 fuselage to be refurbished and retained are the pressure cell and tail assembly – everything else including the cabin pressure floor, pannier area, wings and undercarriage are newly designed and manufactured. The wings will have a larger surface area and redesigned intakes and mountings will house four new Rolls-Royce Germany BR710 engines, which have been adapted to better withstand the harsh and corrosive environment of operating regularly at low level over the sea. Fitting the new engines into the wing bays required a considerable re-design with enlarged intakes to deal with the increased airflow of the larger diameter powerplant. At one point BAe evaluated a 'Nimrod specific' version of the General Electric CF34-8C-34N as an alternative powerplant. It offered the advantage of requiring less redesign of the engine-bay area, but BAe decided to retain the BR710. The BR710 completed its first test in early September 1998 at the BMW Rolls-Royce Development and Assembly Centre in Dahlewitz, near Berlin. The BR710 is also used in the Gulfstream V, but it required considerable modification for the Nimrod and numerous components have had to be made corrosion-resistant. The engines will give enhanced reliability, greater thrust (15,500lb) and lower fuel consumption combined with a 30% larger fuel load that will permit sortie duration in excess of 15 hours without air-to-air

refuelling, though it will retain that capability. Crew fatigue on long sorties, which is the norm for maritime patrol aircraft, is also an important factor and this is helped on the MRA.4 by lower internal noise as the engines are quieter, with less vibration, better sound proofing and modern avionics. It will also incorporate new hydraulic systems, environmental control system, crew oxygen system, automated fuel system, electrical generators and wiring, a new auxiliary power unit plus an improved flight control system.

The new wings' span will be 12 feet greater, creating a 23% increase in area over the original MR.2 wing. It will also incorporate four hardpoints wired to allow the carriage of a variety of external weapons including Harpoon, ATARM, ASRAAM, SLAM-ER, Maverick, Sidewinder and Storm Shadow, thus giving the aircraft an impressive offensive capability. (ASRAAM and Sidewinder are to be trialled later in the development programme). Another significant difference with the news wing are the much larger air intakes provided for the four R-R Germany BR710 high-bypass turbofan engines, each one providing some 15,500lbs of static thrust. These modern high technology modular engines will provide 25% more thrust than the old R-R Spey engines whilst using 30% less fuel. Other external differences between the MR.2 and MRA.4 include a teardrop shaped fairing on the port side of the forward fuselage housing a ram-air turbine. On the base of the fin, is a single inlet for the environmental control system, replacing two inlets on the rear fuselage on the MR 2. The new 'all-glass' cockpit incorporates a new style flight deck using automated flight systems, based on modified Airbus 340 technology, allowing two pilot operation without the flight engineer and route navigator currently required by the MR.2. Inside the fuselage, and linked by MIL-STD 1553B databusses, is a Tactical Command System developed by Boeing from their TMS-2000 system using fibre optics. The Tactical Command System is a powerful data distribution and display programme, using a 'Windows' based operating system that will allow data to be displayed on seven reconfigurable high-resolution multifunctional workstations. The sensors include the new Thales (previously Racal) Searchwater 2000MR multimode search radar that can provide pulse Doppler modes for air to air search and Synthetic Aperture Radar for ground mapping and Inverse Synthetic Aperture Radar for identifying targets. The fuselage houses the eight 'mission crew' which comprise a radar operator, an ESM operator, a communications manager, two tactical co-ordinators, two acoustic operators and one additional dry operator capable of handling either radar or above water communications as necessary. To make the most efficient use of the available manpower some operators are to be cross-trained and additional crew carried depending on the planned mission. For their ASW taskings the aircraft has been fitted with the CDC/Ultra UYS503/AQS970 acoustic processor, a development

of the excellent system currently installed on the Royal Australian Air Force AP-3C Orion. To provide an advanced visual search capability, the Northrop Grumman Nighthunter Electro-Optical Search and Detection System has been installed under the nose in a retractable ball turret. Images from any two wavelengths can be fused into a single false-colour image picture for display on the monitors in the cabin. To counter the yaw that occurs when the turret is deployed, 59in (1.5m) composite finlets have been built on to the horizontal tailplanes. Using TV cameras and infra-red sensors, the Electro-Optical Search and Detection System will add significantly to the aircraft's search and rescue and vessel identification capability. Data taken by this equipment will be recorded using the Super VHS format.

Perhaps the most significant item of new equipment on the MRA.4 is the Israeli Elta EL/L-8300UK Electronic Support Measures (ESM) suite – an ultra capable ELINT system. This comprehensive and multi capable package is able to identify and classify an extensive range of radars carried by ships or aircraft and is just one of a number of items of equipment carried by the Nimrod that will give the aircraft a significant ELINT capability and make it a very useful addition to the Nimrod R.1 in that specialised role. Overland and littoral surveillance roles will increase the Nimrod's exposure to anti-aircraft defences, and therefore a fully integrated defensive aids sub-system has been fitted, comprising an ALR-56M(v) radar warning receiver, an AAR-57 missile approach warning receiver, an ALE-50 towed radar decoy, Thales Vinten Vicon 78 chaff and flare dispensers and infra-red countermeasures flares. The communications capability of the MRA.4 will be particularly impressive with five V/UHF radios, incorporating Have Quick II secure communications, two HF radios, a teletype Modem / Link 11 / Link 16 JTIDS data links and SHF SATCOM. The defensive aids sub-system, feeding into the Tactical Command System, will control a radar warning receiver, a missile approach warning system, towed radar decoy, plus chaff and flares.

The 'A' in the designation of the aircraft stands for 'attack' and is well justified as the MRA.4 will be able to carry the same number of Stingray torpedoes as the MR.2 despite having slightly less space in the pannier. As with the MR.2 the AGM-84 Harpoon ASM can be carried internally, along with the ability to accommodate the ALARM anti-radar missile, Maverick and Stormshadow munitions complimented by the ability to drop mines, although as yet no trials are planned. The pannier will be divided into two bays separated by an area between them which will incorporate a sonobuoy tracking sensor, without causing a reduction in weapons carriage capability, which is enhanced of course by the two additional wing hardpoints mentioned above. There will also be two additional sonobuoy launchers, over the four on the MR.2 and the tracking sensor will be capable of handling up to

Opposite page: MRA.4 ZJ518 in primer colours becomes airborne from BAe Warton during one of its many development flights. BAe Systems

64 sonobuoys at a time, including the new Ultra AQS970 acoustic system which is a development of the earlier CDC UYS503 system and is capable of using the full range of sonobuoys – analogue, digital, passive and active. Smiths Industries have provided an Armament Control System (ACS) that allows the control of stores released from the weapons bay and the four underwing hardpoints. The MIL-STD-1760 databus will also allow the Nimrod to 'communicate' with weapons which are currently in the planning stage. So it may be seen that the package of equipment that will be incorporated into the aircraft is extensive, with upgrades to current equipment, such as the Magnetic Anomaly Detector, although in many cases systems will be completely new.

A number of significant problems were encountered during the development and construction of the Nimrod MRA.4 and these have resulted in lengthy programme delays and the in-service date slipping nine years from 2003 to 2012. The inability of FRA/Serco

endurance of over 15 hours, and carrying a much wider range of offensive weapons and is the first aircraft to have a significant ISTAR capability (Intelligence, Surveillance, Target Acquisition and Reconnaissance Equipment ie. thermal imagers and laser target markers etc).

After the initial crews from the operational conversion unit, No.42(R) Squadron, are trained, the first unit to transfer to the MRA.4 will be No.120 Squadron. At RAF Kinloss, considerable work is taking place to accommodate the MRA.4. Due to its eight foot wider main landing gear and 12 foot greater wingspan, the taxiways and aircraft parking bays have to be widened. A new building is also being constructed to house an MRA.4 simulator, while new maintenance bays are also being built. Essentially the MRA.4 is a new aircraft and consequently they have been given new serials, from ZJ514 to ZJ525. They are also appearing in the new standard paint scheme as seen on MR.2s as they go through major servicing. On

Right: MRA.4 PA-02 ZJ518 seen in temporary primer finish at Warton on 17th May 2005. The increase in diameter of the engine air intakes are very evident.
BAe Systems

Opposite page top and bottom: MRA.4 ZJ518 seen on 27th July 2005 by now painted in Camouflage Grey and Light Aircraft Grey.
via BAe Systems and Andy Evans

to complete the initial work on the fuselage created the first delay. Incredibly, it took until 2003 for assembly of the first prototype MRA.4 ZJ516 to be carried out. A further delay was caused when they tried to attach the new wing to the old fuselage. The old MR.2 wings and fuselages were constructed before the days of CAD / CAM and were built in jigs and then mated by tradesmen hammering & filing the metal to fit as necessary – as a result each fuselage was slightly different, in some cases by up to four inches. Consequently, when the new Airbus-built wings, designed on CADDS5 and manufactured with great precision was presented to the old fuselage, unsurprisingly they simply didn't fit. It also probably didn't help that the re-lifed fuselage was designed on a different CAD system, CATIA, and that the teams had used one fuselage to establish certain datum points and then discovered that the next fuselage they worked on was subtly different. When the Nimrod MRA.4 eventually enters service, it will indeed be an impressive and capable aircraft, with twice the patrol endurance of the MR.2 with a quoted range in excess of 6000 miles, an

August 29th 2005 the third Nimrod MRA.4 development aircraft, PA-03 ZJ517, (ex-XV242), successfully completed its maiden flight, taking off from BAe Systems Woodford and landing at Warton after a 75 minute sortie. In late November 2005 the initial Nimrod MRA.4 structural test specimen wingset and fuselage were delivered to BAe Systems Brough from Woodford. The wingset is referred to as 'PA56', and was originally destined for PA-04; and the fuselage 'tube' which is required to make the testing representative, is quite possibly from AEW.3 XV263. With continued cutback to defence budgets, and despite its promise and the commitment of the Government of the day, whether the MRA.4 will reach full squadron service remains a debate outside the remit of this book, Only time will tell!

Chapter 3: **NIMRODS AT WAR**

The Falklands

When Argentina invaded the Falkland Islands in 1982 the UK military was galvanised into action, and a task force hastily drawn together in order to recapture this remote outpost in the South Atlantic. For long range surveillance and search and rescue in the absence of a dedicated AEW platform the RAF thankfully had the Nimrod. For the Nimrod force there were two immediate requirements – firstly to get aircraft to Ascension Island in order at least to provide maritime cover to the ships and aircraft operating from that base during the build-up, and then to modify these aircraft to meet the exceptional operational circumstances they were about to encounter. The first requirement was met by the rapid dispatch of Nimrod MR.1s from No.42 Squadron to provide air cover around Ascension Island from 6th April 1982 onwards, until the more capable MR.2s from RAF Kinloss, especially MR.2Ps fitted with air-to-air refuelling probes, could arrive and extend the operational radius down to the theatre of war, some 4,000 miles south. The first of the No.42 Squadron MR.1s made their way to Ascension Island, via Gibraltar, without air-to-air refuelling, under the command of Wing Commander Baugh, the Officer Commanding No.42 Squadron who remained as Nimrod Detachment Commander until being relieved by Wing Commander David Emmerson on 22nd April. On the subject of air-to-air refuelling, the RAF's Nimrods projected refuelling capabilities had already reached a fairly advanced stage by 1982 and was thereby rapidly accelerated during the build up to the recapture of the Falklands. In fact there had been a debate in Parliament concerning Nimrod's air-to-air refuelling capability in March 1982, and in April, the month Argentina invaded, and the sailing of the first Task Force ships, British Aerospace had been asked to carry out an investigation into an in-flight refuelling capability for the aircraft. As noted this was then put into accelerated progress and on 14th April 1982 an Instruction to Proceed on Nimrod air-to-air refuelling was received by BAe at Woodford. By 18th April plan drawings completed, and on 27th April XV229 made the first flight with the air-to-air refuelling fit installed. On 30th April dry contacts were made with a Victor tanker, swiftly followed by a wet contact, and the first air-to-air refuelling equipped aircraft was delivered on 1st May. During the 2nd May the system was Service Released for daylight operations, and on 3rd May it was further released for night use. On the 6th May XV238 made a 20 hour flight to prove the system, then next day XV227 flew non stop from RAF Kinloss to Ascension Island to commence duty there. This in-flight refuelling modification consisted of a refuelling probe attached above the cockpit with a fuel hose extending down to the cabin floor. This canvas-on-rubber, flexible bowser hose then ran along the cabin floor for two-thirds the length of the fuselage. The fitting involved the loss of the pilot's escape hatch on the roof of the cockpit and added slightly to flight-deck noise. The rest of the crews soon got used to tripping over bowser hose running along the floor of the fuselage but looked forward to the introduction of more sophisticated under floor plumbing! Pilots say that, if anything, the probe-fitted Nimrods are now more stable directionally than they were before the additions. In all 13 Nimrods were modified during the conflict, and three more were completed afterwards. The first air-to-air refuelling mission for a Nimrod from Wideawake airfield on Ascension Island took place on 9th May utilising XV227 and on 15th May, a Nimrod flew 8,453 miles, the longest distance flown by an aircraft during the conflict. In theory the range of an air-to-air refuelling equipped Nimrod is in the order of 12,000 miles. Its endurance is not limitless, because other fluids, such as lubricating oils, have to be topped up; and with all the comforts in the world the matter of crew fatigue still has to be taken into account.

The Nimrod presence during the Falklands war was built up from the first hastily dispatched MR.1's of No. 42 Squadron to a nominal strength of four MR.2s on any given day. The continuing arrival of MR.2s with air-to-air refuelling probes meant that the aircrafts' influence on the proceedings gradually spread from the Ascension Island patrols of about 400 miles radius to the very long sorties to the Falklands themselves, and beyond. The growing list of tasks included the flying of search and rescue cover for the RAF Harrier GR.3s being flown south to HMS *Hermes* and very importantly, cover and assistance for the 'Black Buck' Vulcan bombing raids on Port Stanley airfield with their Victor and Hercules tankers. Many records were claimed and earned and it's a tribute to the crews and aircraft that none of those they were tasked to look after met with disaster over that huge and featureless expanse of ocean.

Two of the major incidents of the war for the Nimrod force are worth recounting. Firstly, was the initial sighting on the 12th May of an Argentine Boeing 707 reconnaissance jet by a Nimrod of No.201 Squadron whilst providing surveillance for the Task Force. Soon after the aircraft reached 35 degrees south the crew went to Action Stations after detecting Russian Bear D's carrying out a normal peacetime mission. A little later the Argentinean 707 was again detected. The Nimrod maintained its heading until the 707 changed

An unidentified MR.2P undertaking firing trials of the AIM-9P Sidewinder air-to-air missile.

Nimrod MR.2 XV233 drops a Marconi Stingray Torpedo which includes an on-board computer to control the homing system, sophisticated target detectors and the capability to defeat countermeasures.

MR.2P XV232 displaying underwing stores.
All via Andy Evans

direction which gave some indication of the Boeing's range. The lookouts on the starboard side of the Nimrod were straining to see the other aircraft, however the flight deck crew were the first to see it. The first pilot pushed the throttles open as they turned to try to intercept – even though they were unarmed! However it proved to be a lost cause as the Boeing had a speed advantage at that stage. The second notable event occurred on 3rd June 1982 when the 'Black Buck 6' Vulcan Shrike mission captained by Squadron Leader Neil McDougall attacked radar sites at Port Stanley with two of its four anti-radar Shrike missiles. On its way back to Ascension Island some four hours later and whilst attempting to refuel from a Victor off the Brazilian coast its refuelling probe was damaged. By then the Vulcan's fuel tanks were almost empty and the nearest airfield was at Rio de Janeiro, approximately 400 miles west. McDougall, with Flight Lieutenant Brian Gardner aboard as extra pilot and Flight Lieutenant Rod Revaskus in the back, decided to divert to Rio at the risk of internment, and attempted to drop the two remaining Shrikes so as to avoid potential embarrassment to the USA that had supplied them to the UK. However, one of them failed to release. The Vulcan then descended to low level in order to jettison confidential documents. These papers were packed into a weighted navigator's bag and thrown out as soon as the aircraft could be depressurised. They then found that the door could not be closed and it became impossible to climb again to the fuel economy height of about 40,000ft. The door was closed eventually and a rapid landing made at Rio with about 3,0001b of fuel left - insufficient even for one circuit of a strange airfield! During this crisis a Nimrod acted as shepherd giving navigational advice to the Vulcan crew who had thrown out most of their charts and confidential documents. The Nimrod also acted as a long range communications relay station passing diplomatic messages between London and Rio de Janeiro resulting in the correct treatment of the Vulcan crew and their eventual release together with the aircraft.

Other notable missions included a Nimrod MR.2P flying 2,750 miles SSW of Ascension as anti-submarine cover for the main reinforcement convoy on 11th May and an 8,300 mile, 19 hour 5 minute sortie on 15th May to monitor the Argentine Navy and assess any threat to the UK's amphibious forces. On 20th May the progress of the invasion force was watched by a Nimrod of No.206 Squadron with Wing Commander David Emmerson, by then Commander of the Nimrod Detachment, aboard. The aircraft flew a long reconnaissance parallel to, and about 60miles from the Argentinean coast. Other more mundane but nonetheless vital tasks included the constant provision of cover to helicopters and the dropping of mail to surface ships and submarines. During the rapid progress of the war, the arming of the Nimrods with new weaponry took on new impetus, with some work being carried out at RAF Kinloss and RAF St.Mawgan, some at Woodford, with final touches being made at Ascension Island. The installation of the AIM-9P Sidewinders gave the aircraft a self-defence capability as well as the ability to engage Argentinean patrol aircraft such as the Boeing 707s previously referred to. The Sidewinder installations began on 14th May culminating in the first Sidewinder armed flight on the 28th with XV229 flying from Woodford and by the end of June eight aircraft had been modified, six at Woodford and two at Kinloss. A Harpoon installation programme began on 13th April and BAe also carried out a feasibility study for a Martel ASM missile fit. A Harpoon pannier installation was decided upon by 28th April and an invitation to proceed received on 7th May. The first flight of a Harpoon-equipped Nimrod (XV234) took place on 9th June, the first live firing from Boscombe Down being carried out on 11th June, and XV234 returned to service on 24th June. Subsequent aircraft were modified at RAF Kinloss. Further upgrades saw the rapid installation of internal equipment to allow the Nimrod to carry 'iron bombs' thereby giving the aircraft some semblance of a non-standoff anti-shipping capability. Nimrods were also equipped with Stingray torpedoes, still under test at that time.

It is worth noting that Wideawake Airfield on Ascension Island is technically an American base which the UK was able to use. This remote rocky outcrop in the Atlantic Ocean approximately half way between Great Britain and the Falkland Islands offered reasonably comfortable weather compared with conditions further south. Nevertheless living conditions were spartan in what became known as 'Concertina City' and a great deal of ingenuity was required to provide even basic line servicing for an average of four Nimrods on the base at any time. All four Nimrod squadrons sent air and ground detachments to Ascension during the war, with No.206 eventually giving all its Nimrod crews the experience. All aircraft, including the MR.1s of No.42 Squadron, were painted in the newer hemp and light aircraft grey colour scheme.

'Operation Granby' – the 1991 Gulf War

For many months prior to the outbreak of hostilities in the Gulf Region, Nimrod MR.2s and R.1s had been quietly working alongside other coalition forces to enforce a blockade of Iraq's sea lanes whilst listening to the communications emanating from the Iraqi military machine. The MR.2s operated in support of the Armilla Patrol (which was and is the Royal Navy's permanent presence in the Persian Gulf) and proved to be key assets in maintaining the UN economic embargo of Iraq and Kuwait. Initially operating over the Persian Gulf, as 'Operation Desert Storm' commenced, their tasking was soon extended to include the Gulf of Oman, where the bulk of intervention operations took place. In the period up to hostilities the Nimrods maintained a complete surface plot of all merchant shipping in the region and challenged a total of 6,552 ships. They were also instrumental in initiating numerous ship search operations and developing procedures for combat search and rescue. A detachment of three MR.2s was installed at Seeb on the 13th August 1992 to help secure the complete naval blockade of Iraq, as a prelude to the seemingly inevitable war. An unusual occurrence on the 26th of August was a request from a Soviet warship asking for assistance from a Nimrod to intercept a suspected blockade runner! During hostilities two Nimrod sorties were flown each day in direct support of the aircraft carrier USS *Midway* and her accompanying group in the northern Persian Gulf, their primary task was to locate and identify Iraqi Navy surface units and aircraft using Searchwater radar, Yellowgate ESM and IRDS. To aid with self protection the Nimrods were equipped to carry twin Sidewinder missiles and a BOZ-107 chaff and flare dispenser, carried under their wings. After the conflict it emerged that Nimrods had used a towed radar decoy (the GEC-Marconi Ariel) during missions over the Gulf. Nimrods met with considerable success during the conflict making many initial detections and subsequently directing attack aircraft and in particular RN Lynx, onto their targets. The most successful crew was deemed to belong to No.42 Squadron who were credited with assisting in six ship 'kills' and one 'probable'. Additionally, the Nimrod played an important role as an Airborne Command Centre, acting as Scene of Search Commander as part of the search and rescue organisation. During 'Desert Storm' itself they flew 86 combat sorties. An aircraft and crew were held at 90 minutes readiness for 24 hours a day during the conflict and Nimrods participated in two search and rescue operations. Like many of their bomber counterparts, the Gulf Nimrod Force also began to sport some colourful nose-art, most of which was removed on their return to the UK, these ranged from the small 'Battlestar' logo applied to XV244 to the huge 'Muscat Belle' artwork as carried by XV235, and 'Guernsey's Girl' as depicted on XV258. These caricatures added a lighter note to the conflict. The Nimrod R.1s also operating out of Seeb conducted missions similar to the USAF's RC-135 Rivet Joint aircraft.

Bosnia 1988 – 1990

The RAF Nimrods played a full role in the UN led operations over the Balkans, once again providing their particular brand of information and surface pictures as required by the battlefield commanders, this time in central Europe, rather than the harsh climes of the Persian Gulf. The Nimrods MR.2s drawn from the Kinloss wing were based at Sigonella in Italy, to assist in the UN blockade of Serbia and Montenegro ('Operation Sharp Guard'). This duty was shared with US Navy and Portuguese Air Force P-3 Orion's, whilst the R.1s operated from Pincenza.

'Operation Telic' – the 2003 Gulf War

Since the 1993 war the Nimrods had been regularly deployed to the Gulf to continue their monitoring activities as part of 'Operation Southern Watch'. When once again coalition forces were called to action against Iraq in 2003, six Nimrod MR.2Ps from No.206 Squadron were dispatched and manned on rotation by aircrews from the Kinloss Wing . Again operating from Seeb they worked under the aegis of 'Operation Telic', the UKs contribution to 'Operation Iraqi Freedom'. Like other RAF aircraft in the Gulf, six MR.2Ps received valuable system upgrades before hostilities commenced. These included a comprehensive self-defence suite, a WESCAM forward looking infra-red turret under the starboard wing for night time identification and classification of surface ships, a BOZ pod under the port wing, carrying a towed radar decoy and a partial Link 11 system which allowed the Nimrod to receive surface picture data from US warships. These changes came under the unofficial designation MR.2(GM) – GM standing for Gulf Modification. The Nimrods continued the work they had carried out a decade earlier, correlating an air picture and providing surveillance disciplines for the allied forces. Once again aircraft involved sported some inventive artwork, which have become something of a collector's item in the annals of aviation history. XV241 carried 'Guernsey's Girl II', whilst XV235 sported 'Saddam – You are the weakest link – Goodbye', and XV250 had the spectacular 'Maid of Moray'! The Nimrod R.1 was also in heavy demand by the commanders, but details of their secretive missions remain scant.

Afghanistan – 'Operation Herrick'

Since the American lead attacks into Afghanistan following the 9-11 assaults in the USA, the RAF have played a vital role as a coalition partner under the aegis of 'Operation Herrick'. The Nimrods have also played a significant role in these on-going operations in Afghanistan, and it was on one of the many surveillance flights undertaken by the aircraft that a tragedy befell one of their number on 9th September 2006, when XV230 crashed in southern Kandahar shortly before 11am BST after the pilot told ground control that he was facing a serious technical malfunction. It is believed that fire warning detectors went off in the aircraft as flames spread through the fuselage and disabled the controls. A massive short circuit in some of the hundreds of feet of wiring inside the aircraft caused a spark and smoke quickly engulfed the aircraft and claimed the lives of the 14 men on board. Although the Nimrod was flying at 20,000 feet, the Taliban quickly claimed to have shot down the aircraft with a shoulder-launched Stinger missile, however these rounds only have a maximum range of 11,000 feet.

Chapter 4: **NIMROD MARITIME SQUADRONS**

No.42 (Reserve) Squadron

Motto: *Fortiter in re* – 'Bravely in action'.
Badge: On a terrestrial globe, a figure of Perseus – approved by King George VI in December 1938

No.42 Squadron formed at Filton on 1st April 1916 and, after training, moved to France in August with Royal Aircraft Factory B.E.2d and B.E.2e aircraft for reconnaissance duties over the Western Front. In April 1917 the Squadron re-equipped with R.E.8s and moved to northern Italy to cover the Austro-Italian Front, but returned to France in March 1918. In February 1919 No.42 returned to the UK and disbanded at Netheravon, Wiltshire, on 26th June 1919. No.42 Squadron reformed at Donibristle, Fife, on 14th December 1936 from 'B' Flight of No.22 Squadron, equipped with Vickers Vildebeest IIIs and became only one of two torpedo strike units in the UK. After a number of moves the Squadron settled at the new airfield at Thorney Island, Sussex, but relocated to Bircham Newton, Norfolk, on 12th August 1939. It exchanged its Vildebeests for Bristol Beauforts in April 1940 with which it specialised in anti-shipping and mine laying along the coasts of northern Europe. On 18th June 1942 it left for the Far East but was delayed in the Middle East for operations there until December, when it finally arrived in Ceylon. It converted to Bristol Blenheim Vs in India, which were used for bombing missions over Burma from March 1943 but re-equipped with Hawker Hurricane IICs in October for ground attack duties, adding Mk.IVs in November 1944. A change to the Republic Thunderbolt II took place in July 1945, but the Squadron disbanded at Meiktala in Burma on 30th December 1945. It reformed with Bristol Beaufighter Xs at Thorney Island 1st October 1946 as part of Coastal Command's Strike Wing, disbanding again on 15th October 1947. No.42 Squadron's current commission started on 28th June 1952 when it reformed at St.Eval in Cornwall equipped with the Shackleton MR.1 for maritime reconnaissance duties. MR.2s were subsequently received, and the squadron moved to a permanent home at St.Mawgan, Cornwall, on 8th October 1958, where MR.3s were accepted in December 1965. No.42 converted to the Nimrod MR.1 in April 1971 and received the upgraded MR.2s in 1983. No.42 (Torpedo Bomber) Squadron has been involved in numerous overseas detachments and operations, the most significant of which took place in April 1982, when it dispatched two aircraft to Ascension Island as part of the first phase of 'Operation Corporate' – the recovery of the Falkland Islands – gaining its 16th Battle Honour in the process. From October 1990 it provided crews as part of the Nimrod detachment in Oman involved in 'Operation Granby' and in January 1991 provided a major detachment in Cyprus to give further support to the Allied forces. Disbanding as a front-line unit on 1st October 1992 the No.42(TB) Squadron number lives on as the Nimrod training unit No.42 (Reserve) Squadron, formerly No.236 OCU, at Kinloss, Moray in Scotland.

No.120 Squadron

Motto - Endurance.
Badge - Standing on a demi-terrestrial globe, a falcon close - approved by King George VI in August 1944. The Icelandic falcon signifies the Squadron's time in Iceland and its predatory instinct.

MR.2P XV228 in 1997. One of No.42 Squadron's anniversary display aircraft. via Andy Evans

MR.2P XV252 of No.201 Squadron. Displaying a stylised figure '80' on its fin in 1998 to commemorate the squadron's 80th anniversary, following its formation in April 1918. via Andy Evans

Officially formed at Cramlington, Northumberland, on 1st January 1918, No.120 Squadron was intended as reinforcement for the Independent Force in France, but was not declared operational by the time of the Armistice and so remained in a state of limbo until March 1919 when the unit was assigned to mail duties with D.H.9As. Initial runs to France were later supplemented by trips to Cologne, but by October 1919, the British presence on the Continent had reduced and the unit disbanded. The Squadron did not reform until 2nd June 1941, this time based at Nutts Corner, Northern Ireland, and equipped with Consolidated B-24 Liberators flying anti-U-boat patrols over the Atlantic. The units first confirmed success was on 12th October 1942 when U-597 was sunk by depth charges. No.120 moved to Iceland in April 1943, and within six weeks of the move, four more U-boats had been sunk. In March 1944, the Squadron returned to Northern Ireland and joined Coastal Command's massive anti-submarine efforts in support of 'Operation Overlord', the D-Day landings, and by the end of the war, No.120 was the RAF's highest scoring anti-submarine unit with 14 kills. Despite this record, the Squadron was disbanded on 4th June 1945 and not reformed until October 1946 when No.160 Squadron at Leuchars, Fife, was renumbered. Initially equipped with Liberators, these gave way over the coming months to Avro Lancaster GR.3 variants and it was with this aircraft that a flight was deployed to Palestine in November 1947 to assist in the search for illegal immigrants. In 1950, No.120 moved north to Kinloss and prepared for the introduction of the new Avro Shackleton, this being accomplished during 1951 followed by a move to Aldergrove, Northern Ireland, the following year. The unit returned to Kinloss in 1959 and did not finally replace the Shackleton until February 1971. Pooled Nimrods had however become available to No.120 Squadron from October 1970.

No.201 Squadron

Motto - *Hic et ubique* - 'Here and everywhere'.
Badge - A seagull, wings elevated and addorsed - approved by King Edward VIII in May 1936.

This unit can claim to be one of the oldest British military flying units as it can trace its origins back to the formation of No.1 Squadron, Royal Naval Air Service, at Antwerp on 1st September 1914 only to disband on 14th October following the British retreat from Belgium. The unit reformed at Fort Grange on 16th October 1914. Almost immediately the unit was retitled No.1 (Naval) Squadron, and the unit finally crossed the Channel, after a period on coastal patrol duties, during 1915. Its duties were as varied as its aircraft with Avro 504s, Vickers 'Gunbuses', Sopwith Tabloids, Bristol Scouts and other types being used on reconnaissance, photography, bombing and artillery spotting flights mainly around the Ostend/Zeebrugge area. During the night of 6/7th June 1915, Flight Sub-Lieutenant R A J Warneford sighted the German airship LZ37 and set about catching up with the craft. He managed to do so near Bruges, and, after climbing above the ship, dropped six 20lb bombs onto the airship. There was a violent explosion and Warneford later saw the airship in flames on the ground. For this fearless solo attack he was immediately awarded the Victoria Cross. In December 1917, the unit standardised on Sopwith Camels and was soon involved in the mass air-combats of the German offensive of spring 1918. With the amalgamation of the RFC and RNAS into the RAF on 1st April 1918, the unit became No.201 Squadron, RAF and began to concentrate on ground-attack sorties. As with many other units, the Squadron was disbanded on the last day of 1919. No.201 reformed with Supermarine Southampton flying boats based at Calshot, Hampshire, on 1st January 1929 and by the start of WW2 was flying Saro Londons. The following year, No.201 received Short Sunderlands and commenced anti-submarine patrols over the Atlantic until the U-boat menace lessened. The Squadron also joined the successful Channel blockade prior to D-Day and later had the distinction of carrying out the final Coastal Command patrol of the War on 3rd June 1945. The Sunderlands soldiered on, even taking part in the Berlin Airlift. In 1957 the Squadron was disbanded, reforming at St. Mawgan on 1st October 1958 with Shackleton MR.3, moving to Kinloss in 1965. The Shackletons remained until September 1970 when the unit received its first Nimrods.

No. 203 Squadron

Motto - *Occidens and oriensque* - 'West and East'.
Badge - A winged sea horse - approved by King George VI in February 1937

The nascent No.3 Squadron, RNAS, was formed at Eastchurch, Kent, in February 1914 and took its Nieuports and Farman aircraft across to Dunkirk to carry out varying duties in support of Royal Navy vessels in the area. This unit was subsequently deployed to the Dardanelles to provide bombing support in April 1915. During a bombing raid against a railway junction near the Maritza River in Bulgaria on 19th November 1915, Squadron Commander Richard Bel-Davies won the Victoria Cross for landing to pick up a downed pilot in the face of intense enemy fire. At the end of the year, the unit returned to the UK and was disbanded. Six months later, 'C' Squadron, RNAS, based at Dunkirk was retitled No.3 Squadron and the unit flew Bristol and Nieuport Scouts on coastal patrols over the Belgian coast before moving to support RFC squadrons involved in action over the Somme. The unit's number changed to No.203 Squadron at the formation of the RAF. The Squadron saw little change in its duties after the creation of the RAF, remaining in Belgium until March 1919 when it returned home prior to disbanding at Scopwick, Lincolnshire, on 21st January 1920. Reformed at Leuchars in March 1920 as a naval co-operation unit initially with Avro 504s and Sopwith Camels, both types were replaced by the Nieuport Nightjar for carrier-borne fighter duties. No.203 returned to Turkey during the Chanak crisis in 1922 aboard HMS *Argus*, but was disbanded once again in April 1923. On 1st January 1929, No.482 Flight at Mount Batten, Devon, was renumbered No.203 Squadron and the unit moved to Basra in Iraq with Supermarine Southampton's. The aircraft were used for anti-piracy and policing duties in the Persian Gulf and with the arrival of Short Rangoon's in 1931 a number of local rulers were entertained in the capacious cabins whenever trouble was brewing. With war imminent, the Squadron, now equipped with Short Singapores, flew to Aden and converted shortly after to Blenheims. After the Italian declaration of war in June 1940, No.203 became heavily involved in the East Africa campaign before moving on to Crete to cover the evacuation of the beleaguered island. The Squadron flew anti-shipping patrols around the Middle and Far East with a variety of types including Martin Baltimores, Vickers Wellingtons and Consolidated Liberators, remaining in Ceylon until May 1946 when it returned to Leuchars and then St. Eval to re-equip with Lancaster GR.3s. These aircraft remained until March 1953 when the unit relocated to Topcliffe, Yorkshire, prior to converting to Lockheed Neptunes for anti-submarine and maritime patrols over the North Sea. The Squadron was disbanded again in September 1956. On 1st November 1958, No.240 Squadron based at Ballykelly, Northern Ireland, with Shackletons was renumbered No.203. Shackletons were retained until after the arrival of the first Nimrods in July 1971; the last Shackletons being relinquished in January 1972. Based at Luqa in Malta from early 1969, the unit patrolled the Mediterranean until disbanded on the final day of 1977. In October 1996, the Sea King OCU at St. Mawgan was renamed No.203 (Reserve) Squadron, thus returning one of the oldest RNAS/RAF squadrons to active service.

No.206 Squadron

Motto: *Nihil nos effugit* - 'Naught escapes us'.
Badge: An octopus - approved by King George VI in January 1938. Octopus: an active creature, indicating the squadron's vigorous approach to a challenge.

No.6 Squadron, RNAS, was formed on 1st November 1916 as a fighter unit but disbanded less than a year later. No.6 (Naval) Squadron was formed on 1st November 1917 at Dover, Kent, and crossed the Channel with its De Havilland D.H.4s on 14th January 1918, receiving D.H.9s for bomber and reconnaissance duties the following month. With the formation of the RAF, the unit was renumbered No.206 Squadron, RAF, and re-assigned to Army co-operation tasks. Following the Armistice, the unit remained on the continent as part of the air mail service until June 1919 when the Squadron was dispatched to Helwan in Egypt, becoming No.47 Squadron on 1st February 1920.

In June 1936, No.206 reformed, from C flight of No.48 Squadron at Manston, Kent, equipped with Avro Ansons, to provide advanced flying training for newly fledged pilots. A change to maritime patrols over the North Sea during the early days of the Second World War saw the unit involved in action when an Anson of No.206 managed to shoot down an attacking Heinkel He115 floatplane. In December 1939 Anson K6184 bombed a U-boat and succeeded in hitting it, although the latter probably survived due to the ineffectiveness of 100lb anti-submarine bombs. In early 1940, the unit converted to Lockheed Hudsons and moved to St. Eval in 1941 to patrol the southwestern approaches. Two years later, Boeing Fortress IIs arrived and No.206 moved to the Azores to provide convoy protection over a much greater area than had previously been possible. The Squadron returned to the UK in April 1944 and converted to Liberators before taking up patrol duties over the Norwegian coastal areas, a task that the unit continued for the remainder of the War. With the end of the War in Europe, No.206 was tasked with the transport of freight to India and then returning home ex-POWs from the Far East until disbanded in April 1946. The Squadron reformed with Avro York's in late 1947, but disbanded again in August 1949. In September 1952, No.206 Squadron was reformed yet again, equipped with Shackletons, at St.Eval providing reconnaissance and rescue patrols over the western approaches until transferring to Kinloss in 1965. Nimrods arrived in November 1970. The unit was disbanded in a ceremony at RAF Kinloss on 1st April 2005.

No.236 Operational Conversion Unit

No.236 OCU formed on 31st July 1947 at Kinloss with the re-naming of No.6 (Coastal) Operational Training Unit and inherited Lancaster and Beaufighter aircraft amongst other types. With revisions in Coastal Command training and the introduction of the Shackleton, the School of Maritime Reconnaissance (SMR, later to be designated 1 Maritime Reconnaissance School) was formed at St.Mawgan in June 1951 using Lancasters to teach general maritime procedures. No.236 OCU then converted aircrew to the Shackle-

ton Mk.1, and from November 1952 to July 1956 to the Lockheed Neptune also. The two units were combined at Kinloss in September 1956 as an economy measure to form the Maritime Operational Training Unit (MOTU). Amongst other types this unit operated the Lancaster MR.3 for a short time, this period seeing the virtual end of the Lancaster in maritime and indeed RAF service, when Lancaster RF325 was withdrawn in October 1956. During its 14 year life MOTU was equipped with the Shackleton Mk.1, 1A, T.4 (a conversion of the Mk.1A) and T.2 (10 of which were converted from MR.2s) and in the final months of its existence the Nimrod MR.1 was introduced to the unit. MOTU moved to St.Mawgan in June 1965 disbanding on 30th June 1970 and becoming No.236 OCU once more. With the introduction of the Nimrod MR.2 the OCU closed at St.Mawgan on 1st April 1982, reopening at Kinloss as the MR.2 OCU combining with the Nimrod Conversion Flight that had existed since October 1979. On 1st November 1983 the unit returned to St.Mawgan, remaining there until returning to Kinloss on 31st July 1992. With the disbandment of No.42 Squadron, No.236 OCU was renamed Nimrod Operational Conversion Unit No.42 (Reserve) Squadron. No.42 (Reserve) Squadron is thus retained, maintaining the number plate of a 'famous' maritime Squadron.

MR.2P XV241 at Waddington in 1999 bearing the 206 Squadron 80th Anniversary markings applied in 1998 and the Octopus squadron motif. The anniversary markings would remain until removed following the next major service.
via Andy Evans

MR.2P XZ284 also of 206 Squadron seen at RAF Fairford in July 1999 and bearing the same anniversary and squadron motif as seen on sister aircraft XV241 above.
Tim Senior

Appendix I: **NIMROD IN DETAIL**

A range of detail photographs of MR.2P XV230 taken at RAF Lossiemouth.
All Trevor Snowden

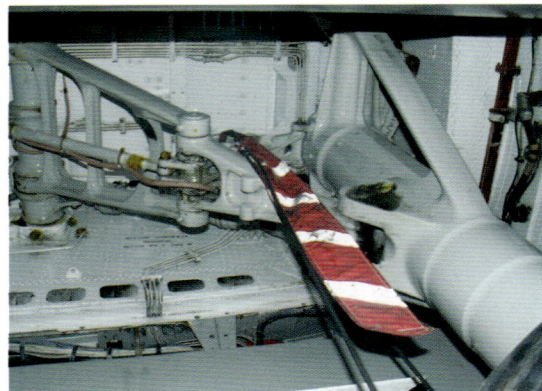

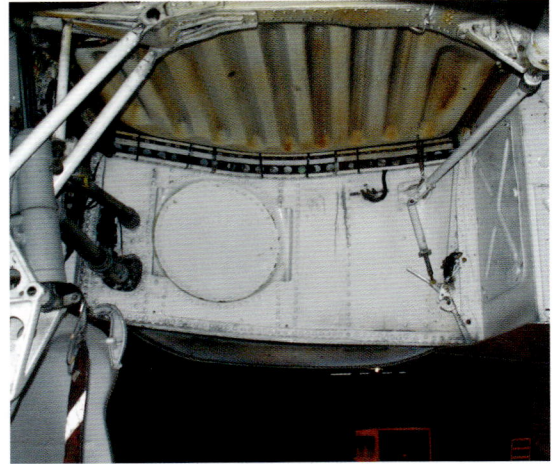

Opposite: *Showing its age somewhat, the flight deck of the Nimrod is still, nevertheless, an impressive place.*
Chris Muir

Above: *MR.2P XV260 at RAF Kinloss in 1994. Although the background tail colour appears in the photograph to be black, it is in fact dark blue.* via Andy Evans

Right: *The port wing of an unidentified MR.2P in the XV serial range which unusually bears the number 295 on the underside of this wing only. Is this a 'zap'? It is not part of any serial number issued to the Nimrod fleet!* Tim Senior

Far right: *XV244 bearing the 201 Squadron motif.* via Andy Evans

Right: *XV226 with 42 Squadron anniversary markings.* via Andy Evans

Above: XV235 top, XV241 centre and XV250 (Maid of Moray), displaying the nose art applied following their deployment to the Gulf region for the war against Iraq in 2003. via Andy Evans

Top right: XV233 displaying 42 Squadron markings and motif. via Andy Evans

Centre right: A 206 Squadron motif. via Andy Evans

Right: R.1 XW664 displaying 51 Squadron motif on fin fillet at Waddington 28th June 1995. Terry Senior

NIMROD MR.1

Nimrod MR.1 XV250, 203 Squadron, RAF Luqa, Malta, 1974.
Light Aircraft Grey overall with white fuselage top decking and vertical tail surfaces; roundels in six positions. Serial in black, repeated below wings; black/white sharkmouth on nose (the latter lasted only a few days and the aircraft was nicknamed 'Smiley'). Unit motif in green on fin fillet; unit badge on forward fuselage.

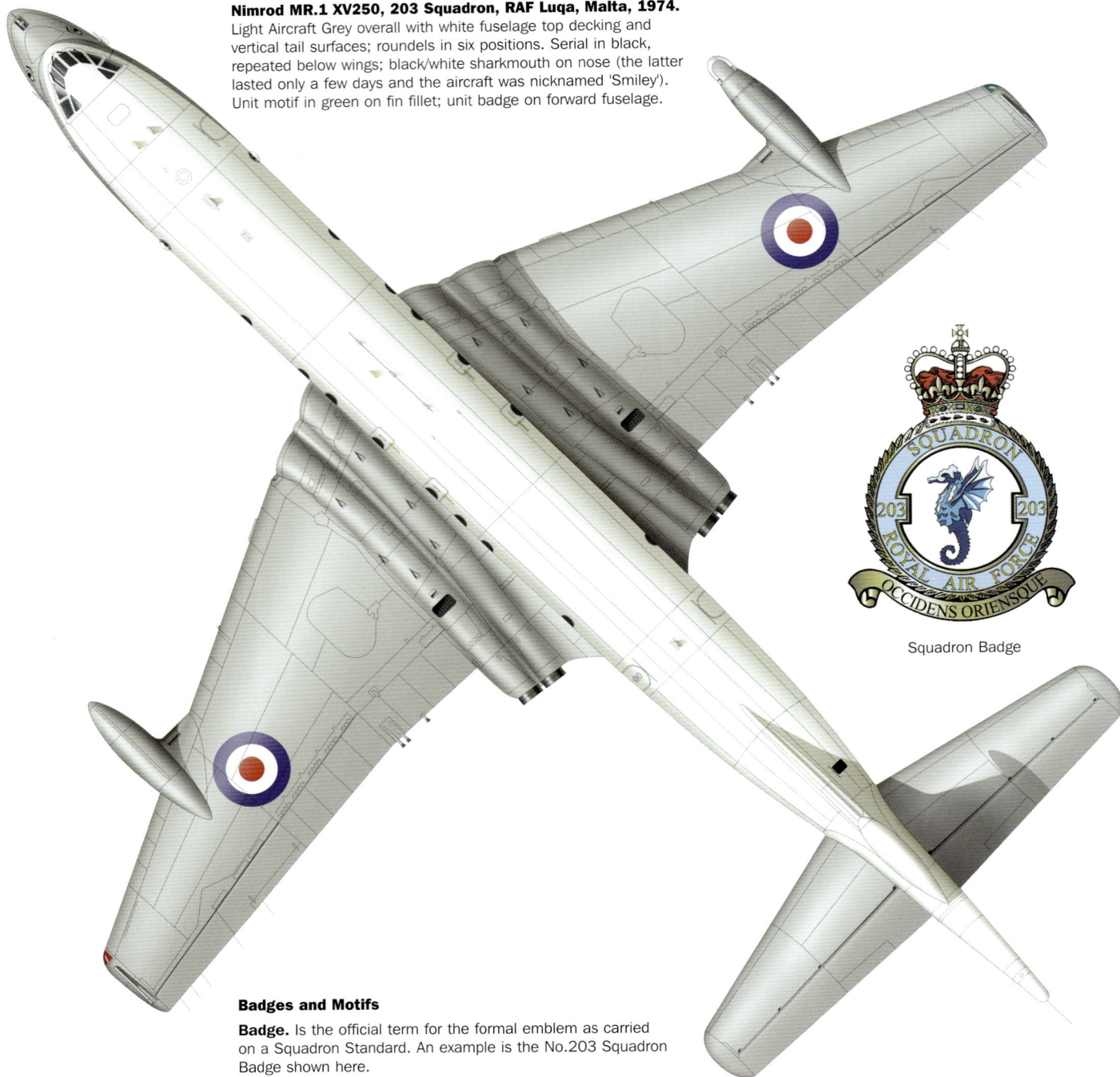

Squadron Badge

Badges and Motifs

Badge. Is the official term for the formal emblem as carried on a Squadron Standard. An example is the No.203 Squadron Badge shown here.

Motif. Used to describe the feature depicted in the centre of the Badge and often used independently as the Squadron marking, as illustrated.

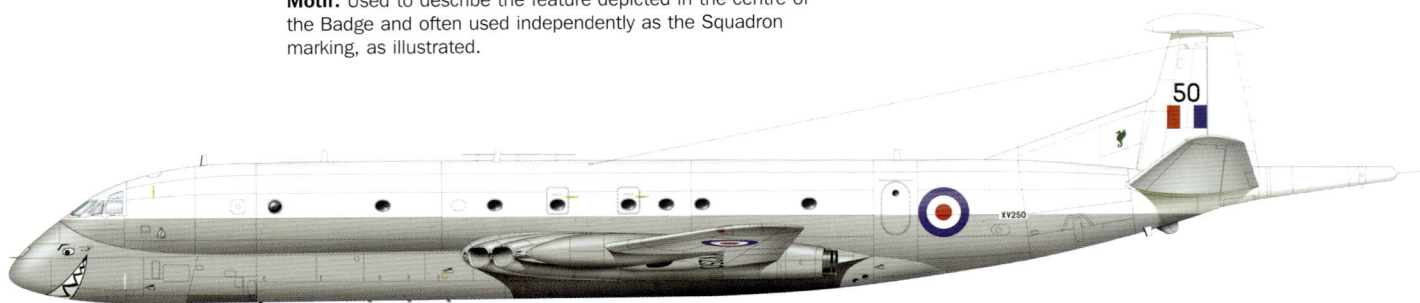

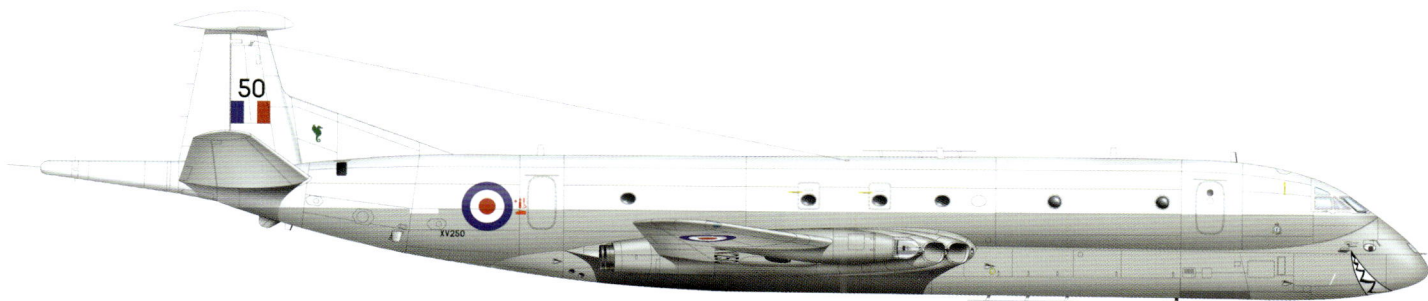

Squadron Motif

NIMROD MR.1

Prototype Nimrod MR.1 XV148, Royal Aircraft Establishment, Bedford, 1981.
Light Aircraft Grey overall with white fuselage top decking; red tail section with white control surfaces and fin tip fairing, red wingtips. Roundels in six positions. Fin flash outlined in white; serials on red section in white.

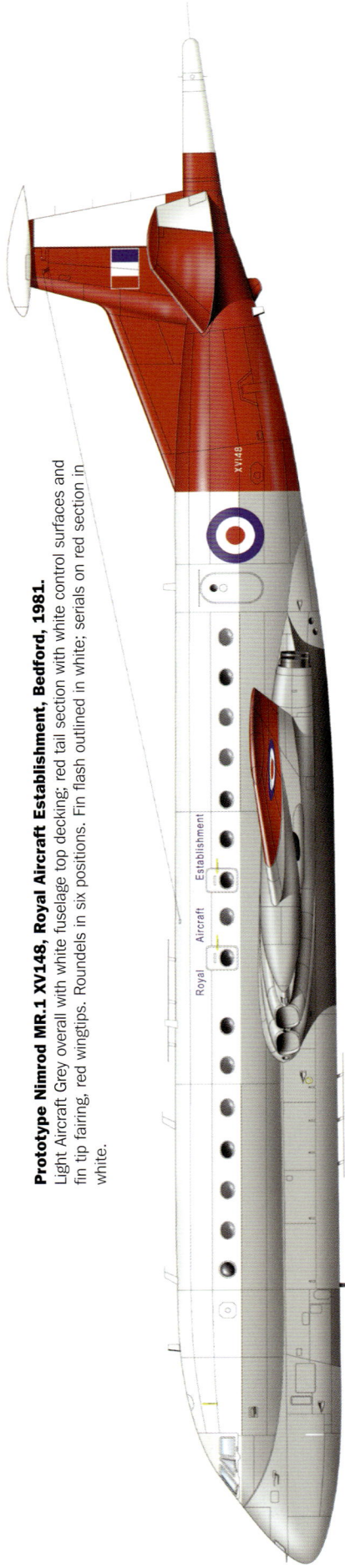

Nimrod MR.1 XV251, 120 Squadron, RAF Kinloss, early 1970s.
Light Aircraft Grey overall with white fuselage top decking and vertical tail surfaces; black serials, codes and nose radar panel. Roundels in six positions; unit badge with Air Marshal's rank panel and yellow/green 'CXX' carried on nose.

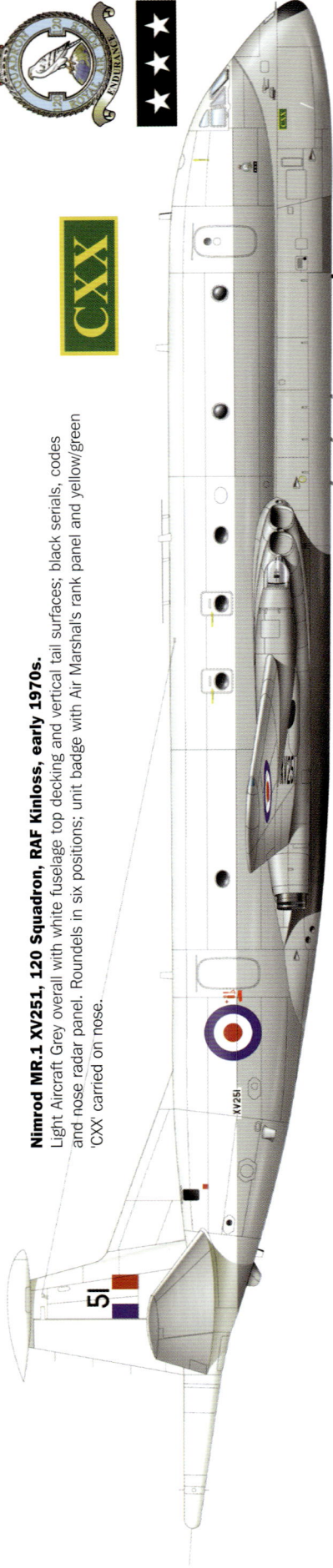

Nimrod MR.1 XV257, 203 Squadron, RAF Luqa, Malta, 1972.
Light Aircraft Grey overall with white fuselage top decking and vertical tail surfaces; black serial and code. Black nose; unit badge added below rear cockpit window. Roundels in six positions.

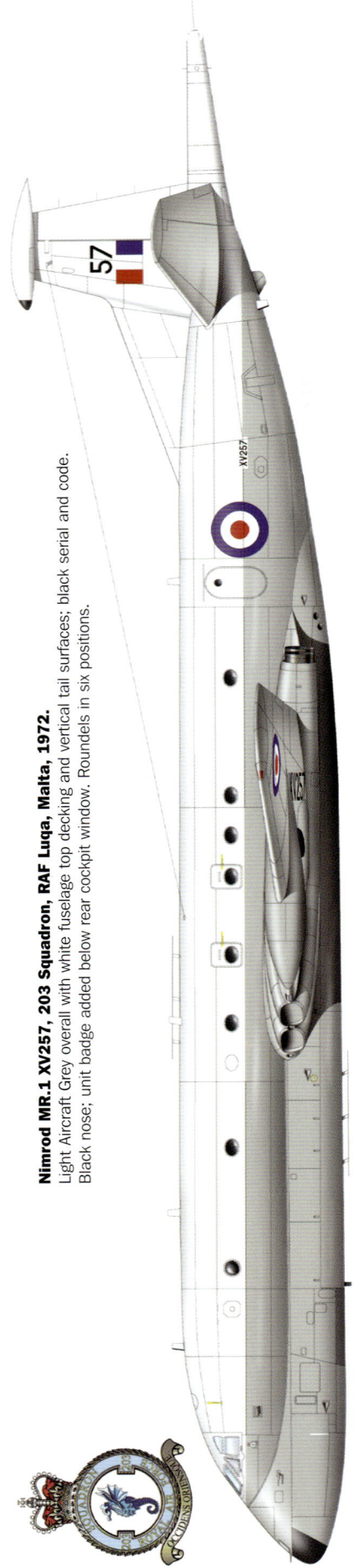

Nimrod MR.1 XV250, 203 Squadron, RAF Luqa, Malta, winner of the Fincastle Trophy November-December 1973.

Light Aircraft Grey overall with white fuselage top decking and vertical tail surfaces; black serial and code. Roundels in six positions; red kangaroo (Australia) and brown buffalo (Canada) 'zaps' on fin fillet; motif in green. Unit badge on forward fuselage. This was the first time that a non-UK based RAF crew had achieved this honour.

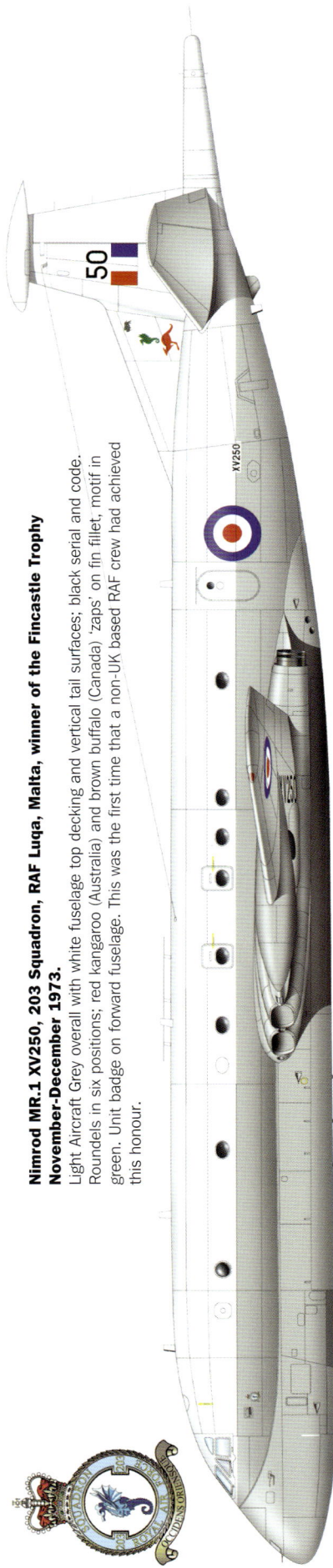

Nimrod MR.1 XV254, 120 Squadron, RAF Kinloss, 1977.

Light Aircraft Grey overall with white fuselage top decking and vertical tail surfaces; serials and codes in black. Unit marking in yellow on a green background, outlined in black, on fin fillet; unit badge on nose on a white rectangle. Roundels in six positions.

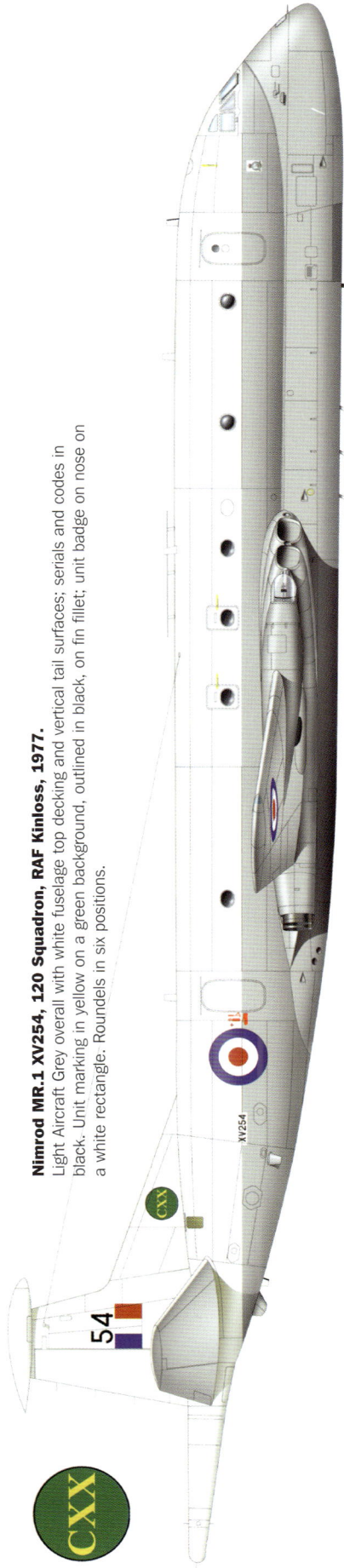

Nimrod MR.1 XV259, 206 Squadron, RAF Kinloss, summer 1977.

Light Aircraft Grey overall with white fuselage top decking and vertical tail surfaces; serials and codes in black. Roundels in six positions; unit motif within a blue circle on fin fillet, unit badge on a white rectangle on forward fuselage.

Nimrod MR.1 XV256, 206 Squadron, RAF Kinloss, 1978.

Light Aircraft Grey overall with white fuselage top decking, fin and rudder; black serial and code. Unit motif on fin fillet, unit badge on forward fuselage; red kangaroo ahead of unit motif denoting participation in the Fincastle Trophy. Roundels in six positions. This aircraft crashed following a bird strike on 17th November 1980.

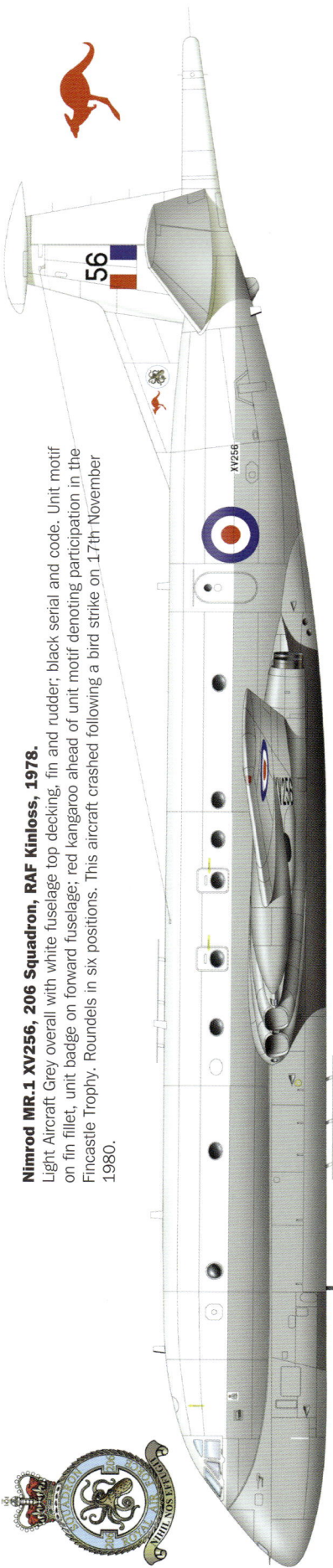

Nimrod MR.1 XV246, RAF St Mawgan Wing, as recorded at Malta in October 1977.

First camouflage experimental finish at the Nimrod Major Servicing Unit, RAF Kinloss, in Dark Earth/Light Aircraft Grey with blue/red roundels on upper surfaces and fuselage, whilst retaining the standard blue/white/red roundels below the wings; serial and code in black. The Dark Earth upper colour was subsequently toned down to become what was later referred to as Hemp.

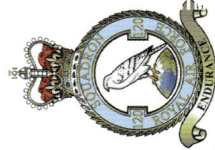

Nimrod MR.1 XV246, 120 Squadron, RAF St.Mawgan, 1978.

Hemp/Light Aircraft Grey finish with black serial and code; blue/red roundels on upper surfaces and fuselage, whilst retaining the blue/white/red roundels below wings. Squadron badge on forward fuselage.
Note: The high camouflage division line aft of the wings, and the extension of the Light Aircraft Grey right up to the nose, unique to this example, has been retained.

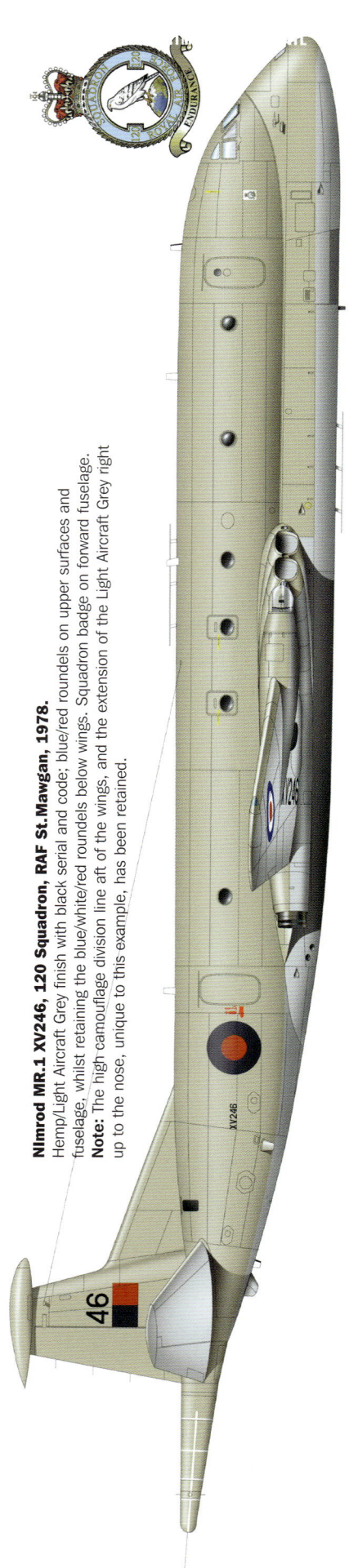

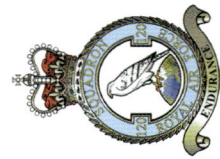

Nimrod MR.1 XV246, 120 Squadron, RAF Kinloss, 1980.
Hemp/Light Aircraft Grey finish with black serial and code; blue/red roundels on upper surfaces and fuselage, whilst retaining the blue/white/red roundels below wings. 'Crew 6' (Fincastle Trophy) marking on fin. Squadron badge on forward fuselage surmounting 'CXX' in gold, over green rectangle.

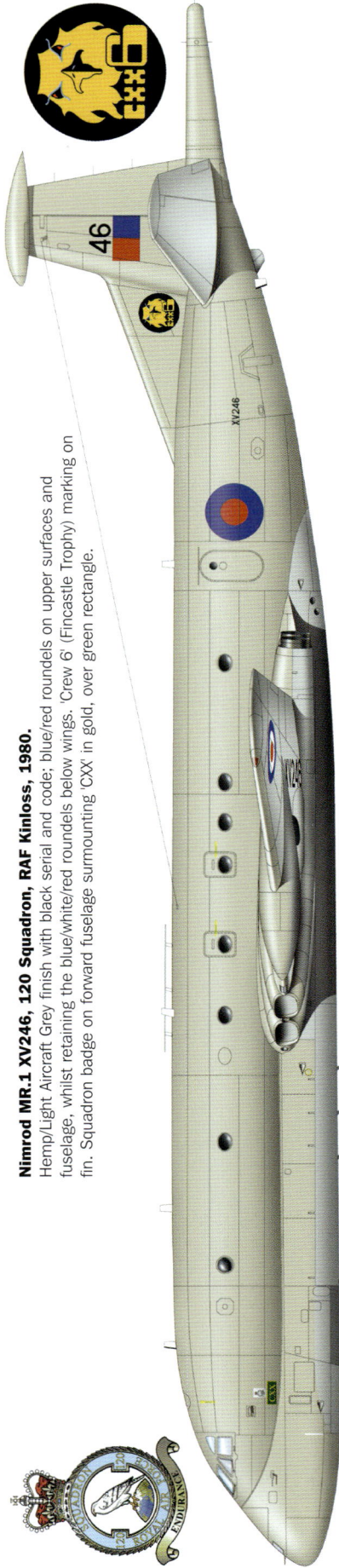

Nimrod MR.1 XZ282, 201 Squadron, RAF Kinloss, 1980.
Light Aircraft Grey overall with white fuselage top decking, fin and rudder; black serial and code. Unit motif on fin and unit badge on forward fuselage. Blue/white/red roundels in six positions.

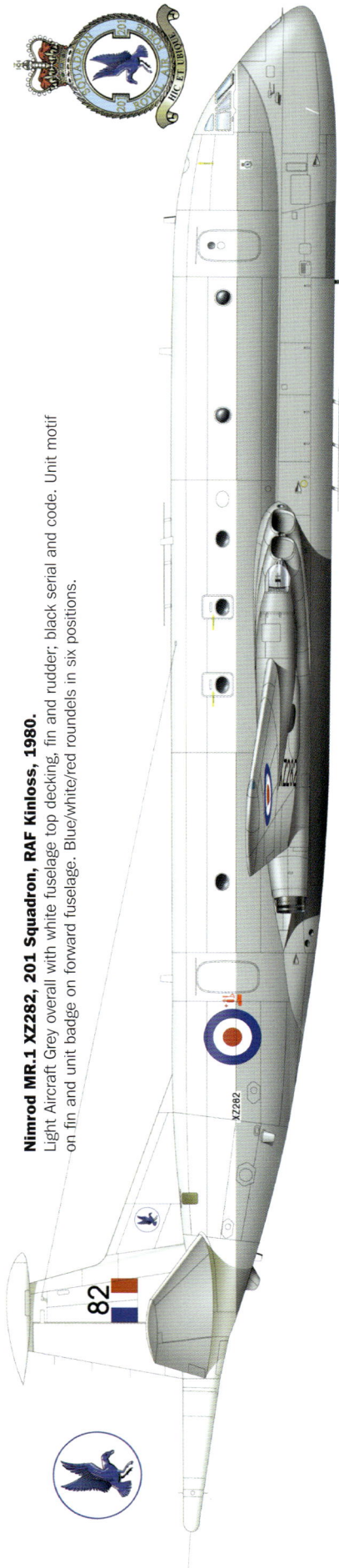

NIMROD R.1

Nimrod R.1 XW666, 51 Squadron, RAF Wyton, 1986.
Hemp/Light Aircraft Grey finish with black serial and code; blue/red roundels on upper surfaces and fuselage, whilst retaining the blue/white/red roundels below wings. Black serial; unit motif on a blue disc, edged in red, on fin fillet. XW666 ditched into the Moray Firth on 16th May 1995.

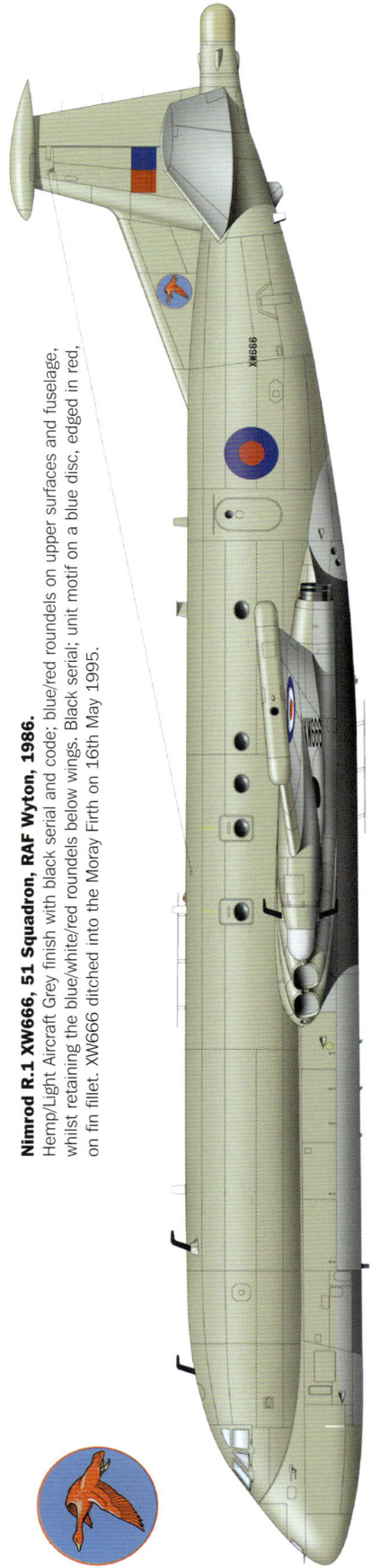

Nimrod R.1 XW664, 51 Squadron, RAF Wyton, 1990.

Hemp/Light Aircraft Grey finish; full size pale blue/red roundels on upper surfaces, fuselage and pale blue/red fin flash. Standard full colour blue/white/red roundels retained below wings. Black serial; unit motif within a red circle on fin fillet.

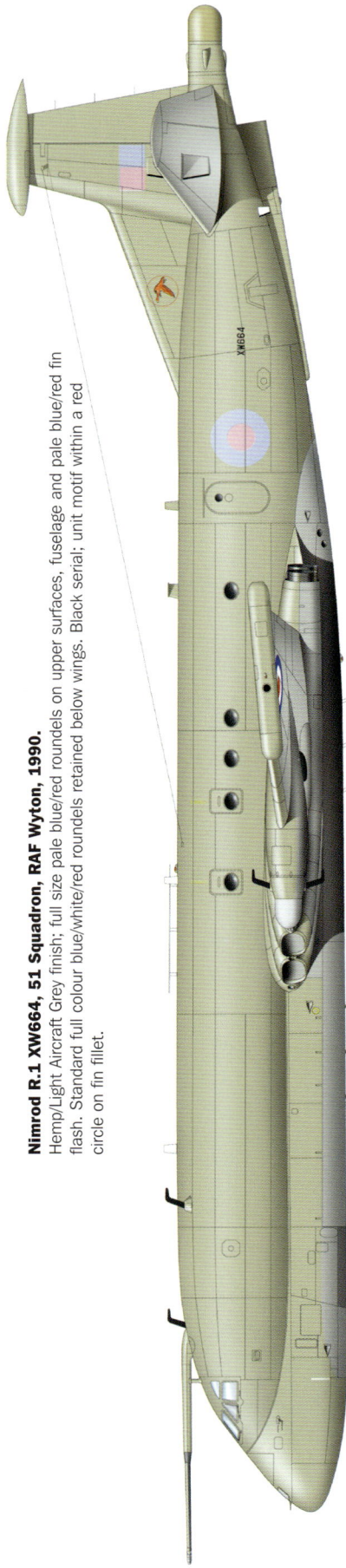

Nimrod R.1 XW664, 51 Squadron, RAF Wyton, 1996.

Hemp/Light Aircraft Grey finish; small diameter pale blue/red roundels in six positions, fin flash in the same colour also reduced in size. White serial. Unit motif (no background) on fin in yellow.

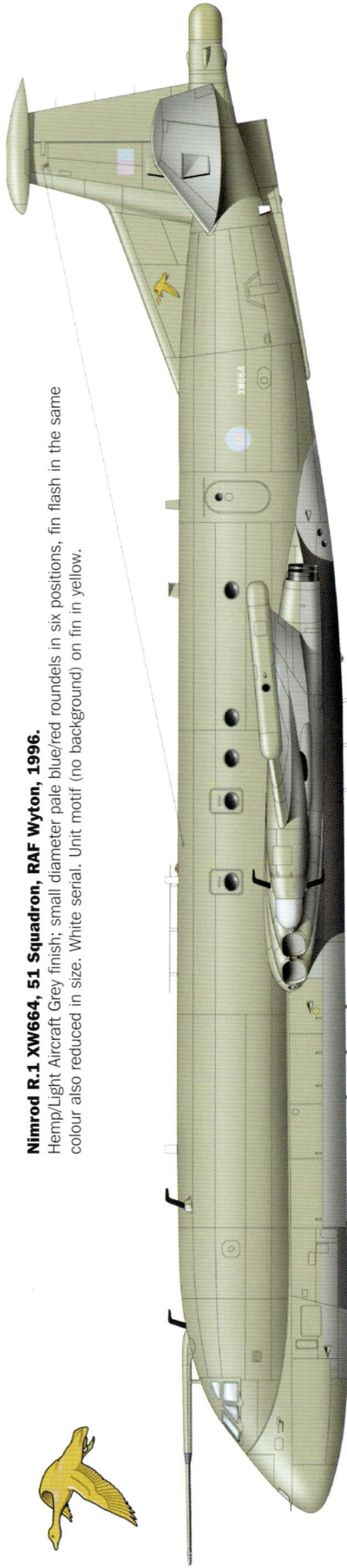

Nimrod R.1 XW665, 51 Squadron, RAF Waddington, 2005.

Camouflage Grey overall with Light Aircraft Grey fuselage top decking; serial in white. Pale blue/red roundels in six positions. Unit motif in red on fin fillet; RAF Waddington shield aft of cockpit.

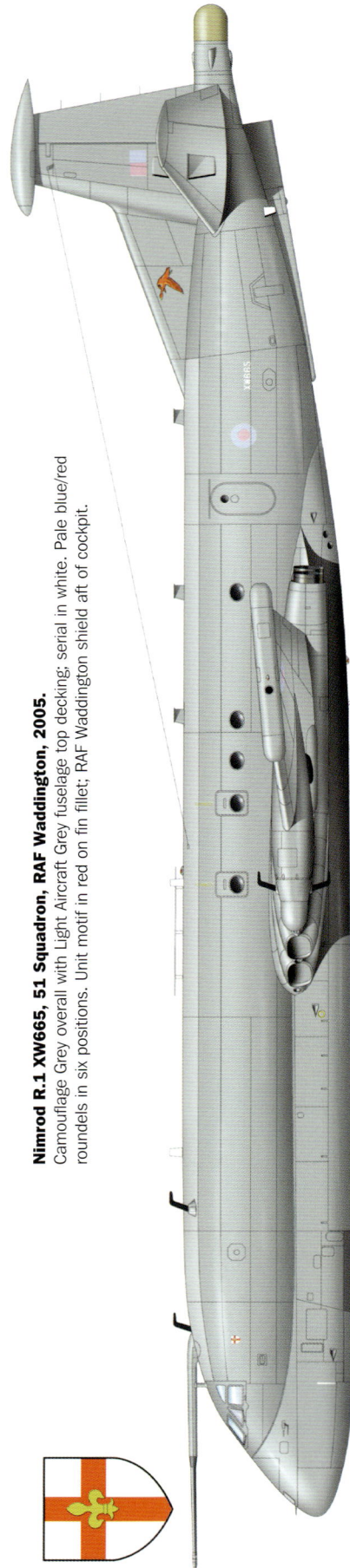

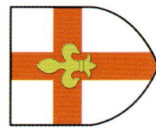

Nimrod R.1 XV249, 51 Squadron, RAF Waddington, 2005.
Camouflage Grey overall with Light Aircraft Grey fuselage top decking; white serial. Pale blue/red roundels in six positions; unit motif on fin fillet, Waddington shield on forward fuselage

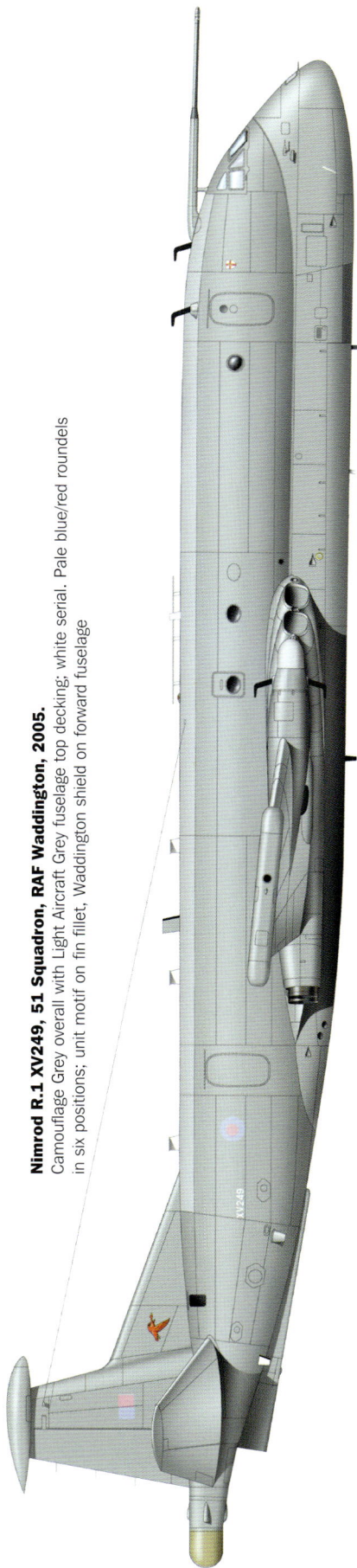

NIMROD MR.2

Nimrod MR.2 XV258, 42 Squadron, RAF St.Mawgan, 1983.
Hemp/Light Aircraft Grey finish with black serial and code (on fin and nose); blue/red roundels on upper surfaces and fuselage, whilst retaining blue/white/red roundels below wings. Station and unit badges on nose within white shields.

Nimrod MR.2 XV229, Kinloss Wing, 1984.
Hemp/Light Aircraft Grey finish with black serial and codes (fin and nose); blue/red roundels on upper surfaces and fuselage, whilst retaining blue/white/red roundels below wings. Fincastle Trophy winner, with special artwork on fin as shown in detail (flags consist of the Union Flag, and those of Australia, Canada and New Zealand).

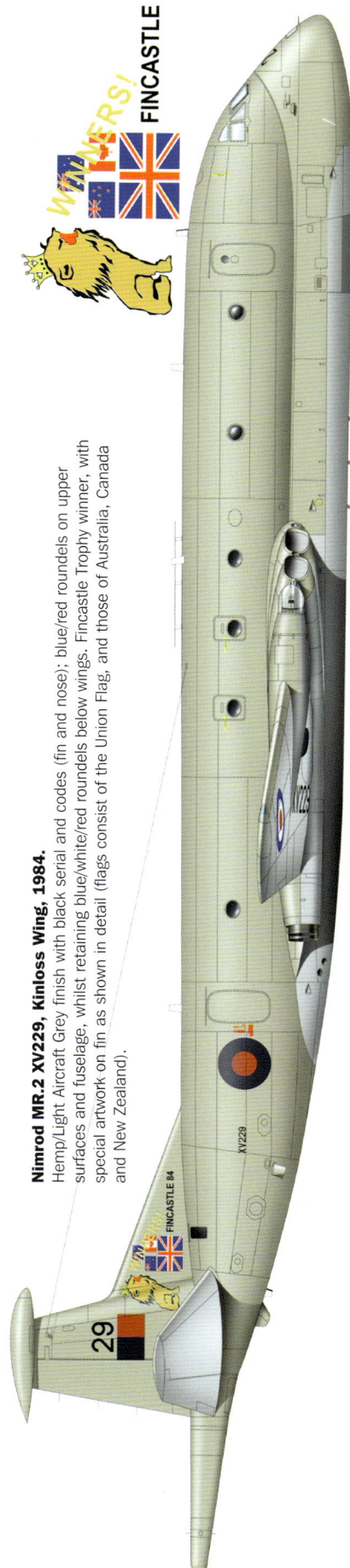

FINCASTLE 84

Nimrod MR.2 XV227, Wideawake, Ascension Island.
Hemp/Light Aircraft Grey finish with black serial and code; blue/red roundels on upper surfaces and fuselage, whilst retaining blue/white/red roundels below wings.

Sidewinders can be carried asymmetrically as illustrated here or symmetrically with either one or two missiles per wing.

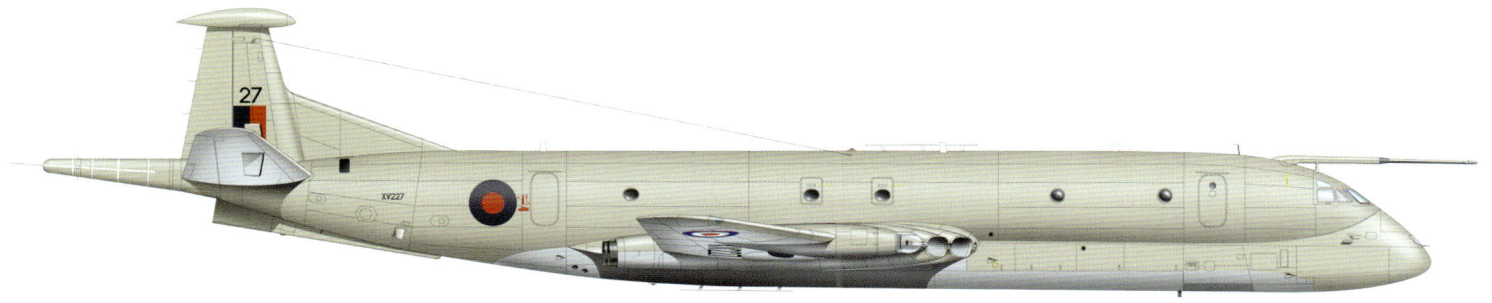

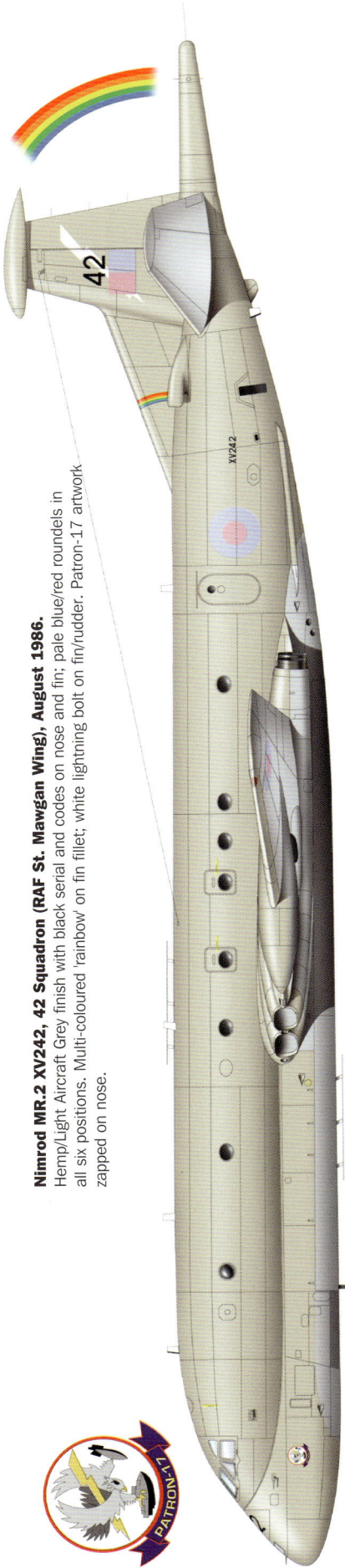

Nimrod MR.2 XV242, 42 Squadron (RAF St. Mawgan Wing), August 1986.
Hemp/Light Aircraft Grey finish with black serial and codes on nose and fin; pale blue/red roundels in all six positions. Multi-coloured 'rainbow' on fin fillet; white lightning bolt on fin/rudder. Patron-17 artwork zapped on nose.

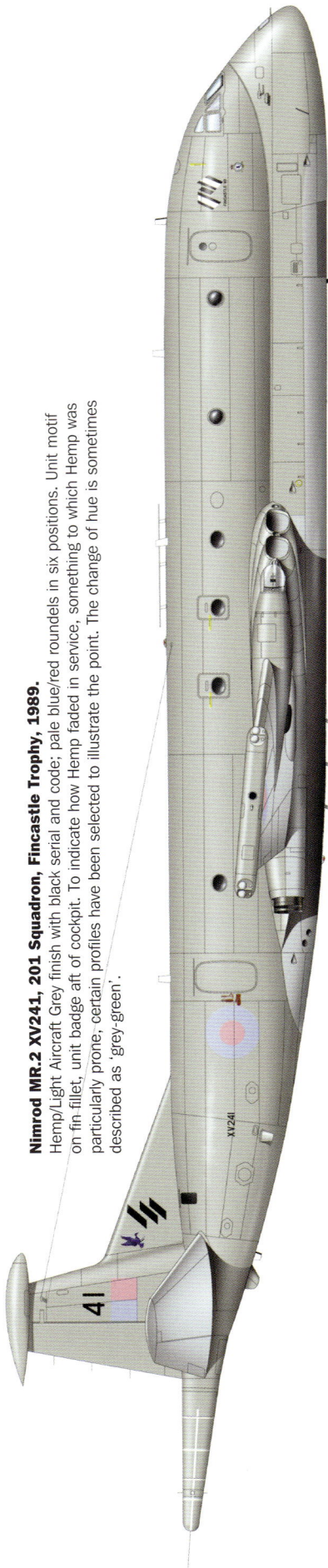

Nimrod MR.2 XV241, 201 Squadron, Fincastle Trophy, 1989.
Hemp/Light Aircraft Grey finish with black serial and code; pale blue/red roundels in six positions. Unit motif on fin fillet, unit badge aft of cockpit. To indicate how Hemp faded in service, something to which Hemp was particularly prone, certain profiles have been selected to illustrate the point. The change of hue is sometimes described as 'grey-green'.

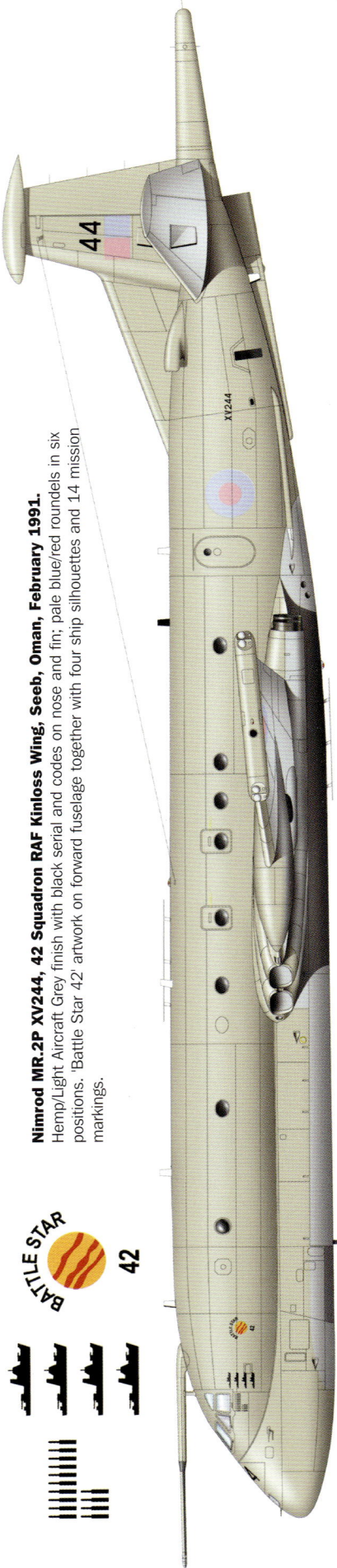

Nimrod MR.2P XV244, 42 Squadron RAF Kinloss Wing, Seeb, Oman, February 1991.
Hemp/Light Aircraft Grey finish with black serial and codes on nose and fin; pale blue/red roundels in six positions. 'Battle Star 42' artwork on forward fuselage together with four ship silhouettes and 14 mission markings.

BATTLE STAR
42

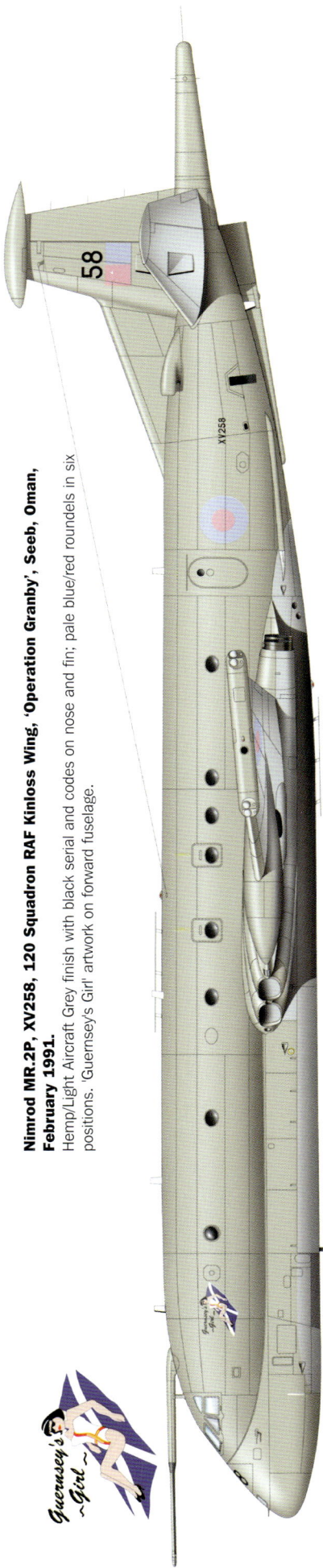

Nimrod MR.2P, XV258, 120 Squadron RAF Kinloss Wing, 'Operation Granby', Seeb, Oman, February 1991.

Hemp/Light Aircraft Grey finish with black serial and codes on nose and fin; pale blue/red roundels in six positions. 'Guernsey's Girl' artwork on forward fuselage.

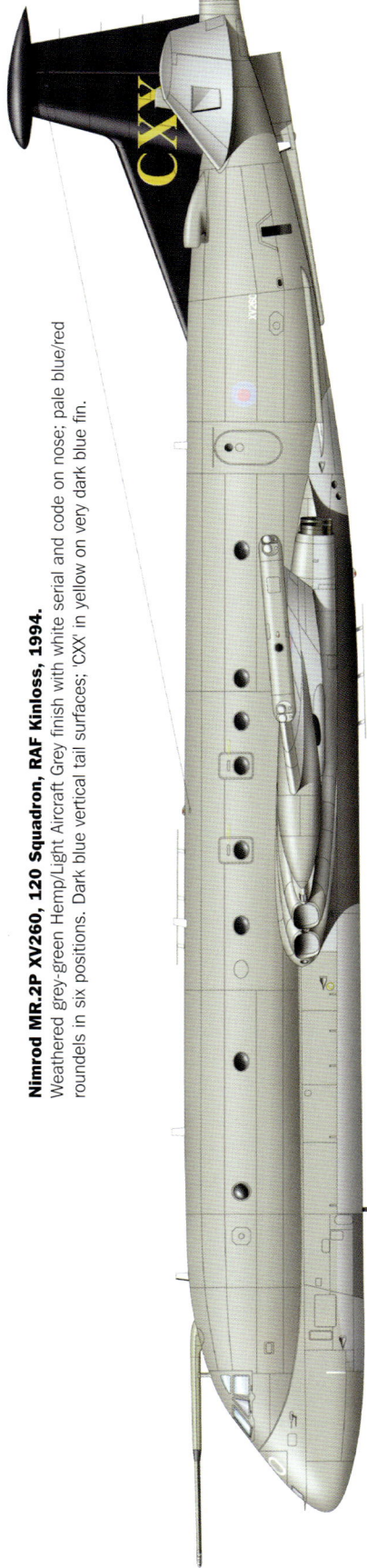

Nimrod MR.2P XV260, 120 Squadron, RAF Kinloss, 1994.

Weathered grey-green Hemp/Light Aircraft Grey finish with white serial and code on nose; pale blue/red roundels in six positions. Dark blue vertical tail surfaces; 'CXX' in yellow on very dark blue fin.

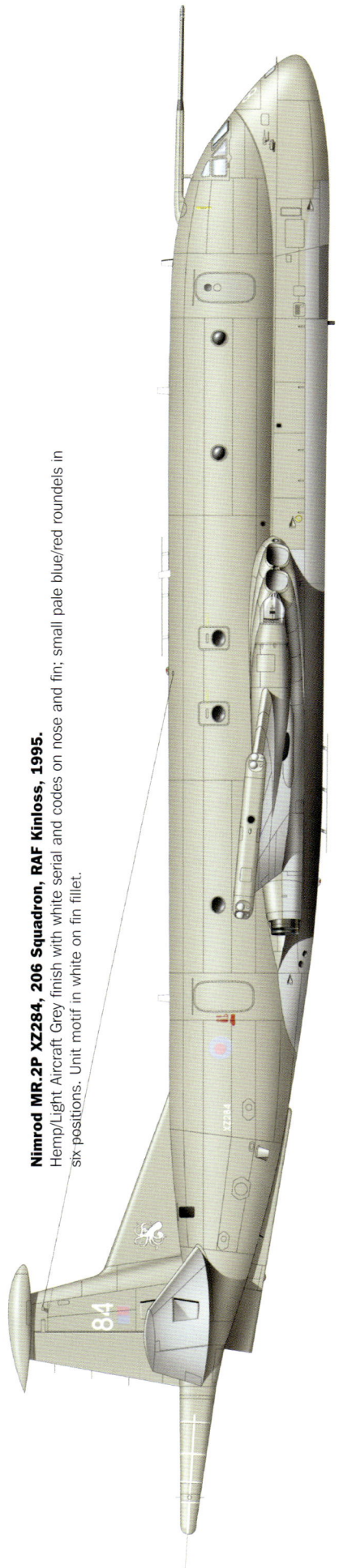

Nimrod MR.2P XZ284, 206 Squadron, RAF Kinloss, 1995.

Hemp/Light Aircraft Grey finish with white serial and codes on nose and fin; small pale blue/red roundels in six positions. Unit motif in white on fin fillet.

Nimrod MR.2P XV233, 42 Squadron, 1997.
Hemp/Light Aircraft Grey finish with white serial and code on nose; pale blue/red roundels in six positions. Bright blue vertical tail surfaces with yellow '42' outlined in white and unit motif. Note the unusual wide space that appears between the letters and numerals of the serial.

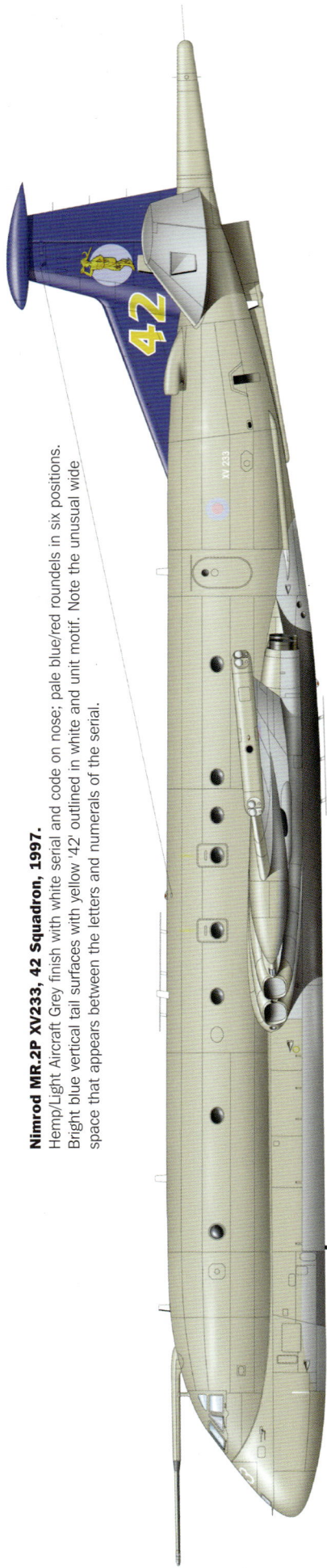

Nimrod MR.2P XV252, 201 Squadron, No. 201 Squadron, RAF Kinloss, 1998.
Hemp/Light Aircraft Grey finish with white serial and code on nose; pale blue/red roundels in six positions. Unit motif in light and dark blue on fin; red '80' denoting the unit's 80th anniversary – formed 1st April 1918 – on fin, outlined in white.

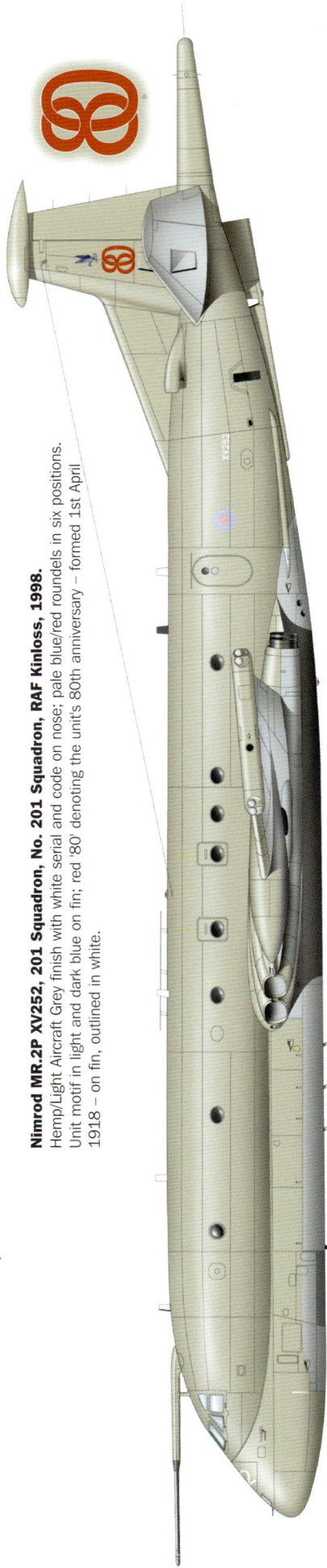

Nimrod MR.2P XV241, 206 Squadron, 1999.
Weathered grey-green Hemp/Light Aircraft Grey finish with white serial and code on nose; pale blue/red roundels in six positions. Bright blue vertical tail surfaces and white '206' on fin with thin black inner offset path. Unit motif on fin.

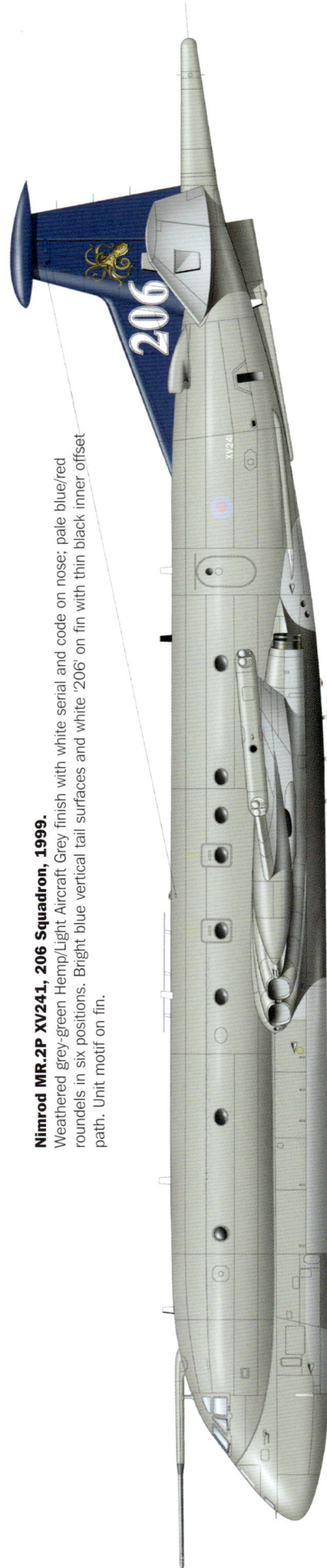

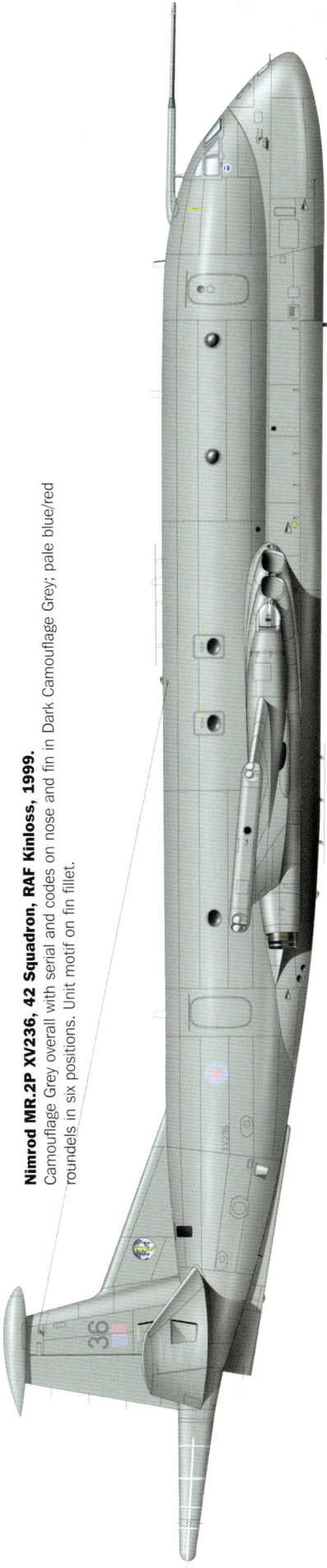

Nimrod MR.2P XV236, 42 Squadron, RAF Kinloss, 1999.
Camouflage Grey overall with serial and codes on nose and fin in Dark Camouflage Grey; pale blue/red roundels in six positions. Unit motif on fin fillet.

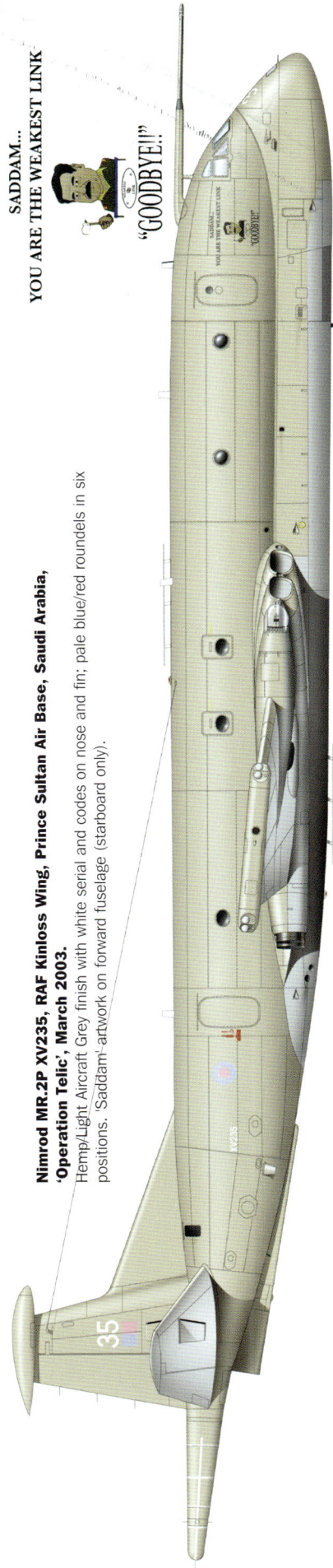

Nimrod MR.2P XV235, RAF Kinloss Wing, Prince Sultan Air Base, Saudi Arabia, 'Operation Telic', March 2003.
Hemp/Light Aircraft Grey finish with white serial and codes on nose and fin; pale blue/red roundels in six positions. 'Saddam'-artwork on forward fuselage (starboard only).

SADDAM...
YOU ARE THE WEAKEST LINK
"GOODBYE!"

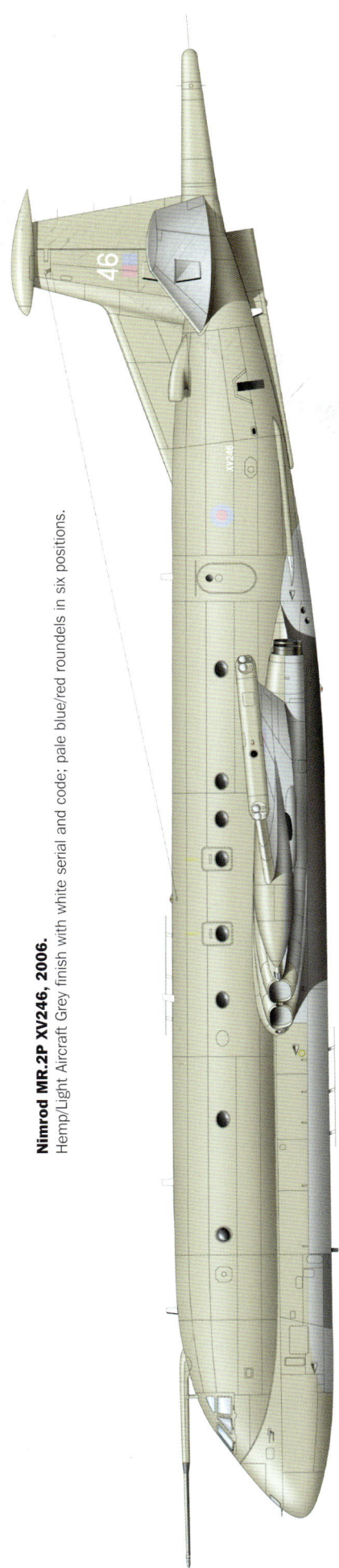

Nimrod MR.2P XV246, 2006.
Hemp/Light Aircraft Grey finish with white serial and code; pale blue/red roundels in six positions.

Nimrod AEW.3 Prototype, DB1 XZ286, RAF Waddington, July 1980 (first flight).
Light Aircraft Grey overall with white fuselage top decking, fin and rudder; black serial. Red/white/blue roundels in six positions.

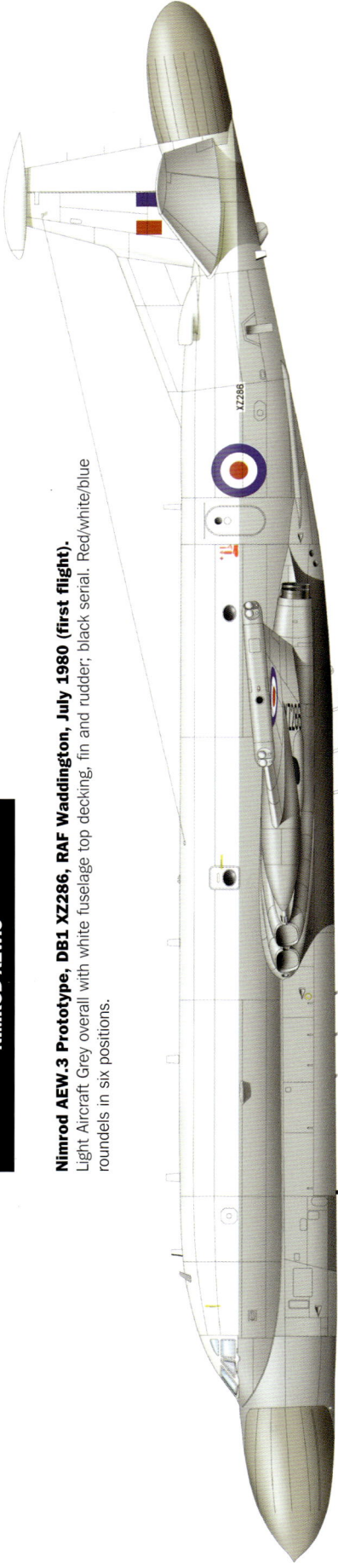

Nimrod AEW.3 P3 XV263, RAF Waddington, 1986.
Hemp /Light Aircraft Grey finish with black serial and code. Blue/red roundels in six positions.

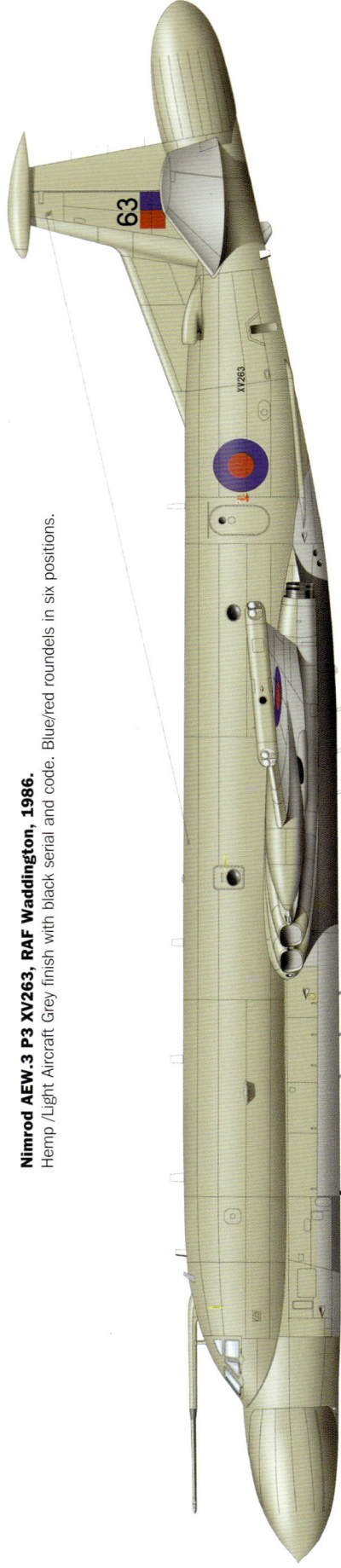

Nimrod AEW.3 XZ285, RAF Waddington.
Weathered grey-green Hemp/Light Aircraft Grey finish with black serial and code. Blue/red roundels on upper surfaces and fuselage, whilst retaining blue/white/red roundels below wings. Waddington shield on forward fuselage, starboard side only.

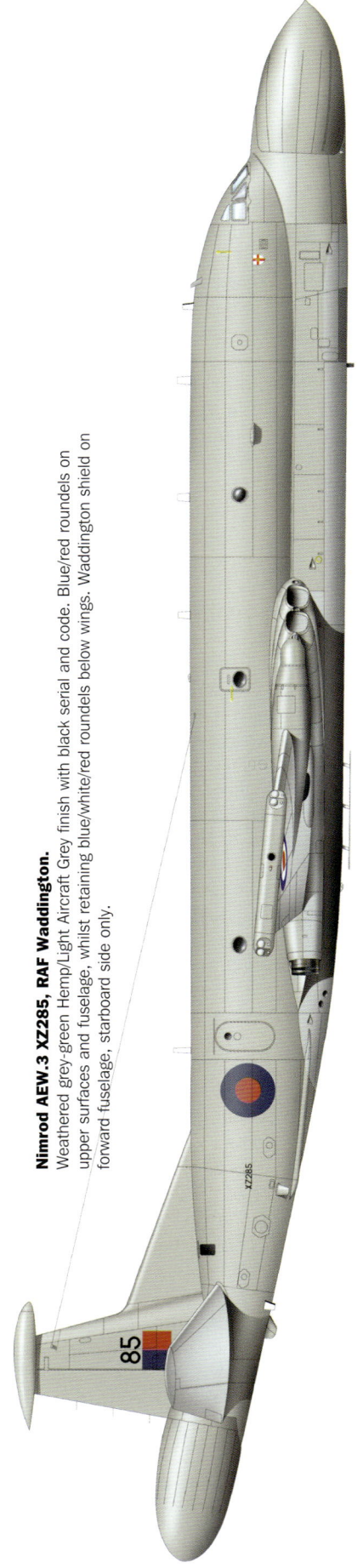

Appendix II: **NIMROD IN CONCLUSION**

The saga of delays that have dogged the introduction to service of the Nimrod MRA.4 has had a serious knock-on effect to the continuing serviceability of the existing Nimrod MR.2s. The projected in service date for the new Nimrod has continually been pushed back, and its numbers consistently culled, as has been indicated elsewhere in this book. This has led many to speculate that although it may have superior sensors and enhanced capabilities, could so few aircraft undertake the demanding roles now foisted on the RAF in the 21st century? The Nimrods original *raison d'être* was to protect UK waters and its assets, yet the MR.2s can now be found undertaking heavily tasked reconnaissance and co-ordination duties in the Gulf and Afghanistan, despite the aircraft's age and continuing concerns about its flight safety.

These concerns were certainly concentrated with the loss of a Nimrod over Afghanistan in September 2006, which caused shock waves throughout the community and gave a platform to many within the armed services to voice their misgivings about the aircraft's safety under these harsh and sustained operational conditions, and to bring forth their own highly volatile stories of incidents involving in-flight emergencies that could have proved catastrophic to aircraft and crews. One crewman told of a hole appearing on the airframe of one Nimrod into which they had to jam an aluminium kettle to maintain the cabin integrity, whilst another explained a similar circumstance when a hole developed in one of the heating pipes causing superheated air to be blasted against the airframe, burning through cabling and metal and damaging the seals around the fuel tanks. Thankfully both aircraft survived. Less than four months after the fatal Nimrod crash the entire fleet was grounded over safety concerns, however due to their heavy tasking they were quickly returned to service, despite continuing fears.

At the time of writing the RAF have still to publish the findings of the Board of Enquiry into the Nimrod crash in Afghanistan, but many continue to believe a fire resulting from a fuel leak during air-to-air refuelling was the ultimate cause, and some anonymous former and current Nimrod engineers have come forward to explain that there are now more faults with the Nimrod than at any other time in its service history with too many instances of equipment failures, engine shutdowns and fuel leaks being reported. In early November 2006 another Nimrod operating in Afghanistan suffered a broken fuel pipe, which could have had serious consequences! Co-Pilot of the ill fated Nimrod, Steve Swarbrick, allegedly told his partner Laura on a number of occasions that he felt there was going to be an accident … and a serious one and that ailing air-

craft had to be cannibalised in order to get the more able aircraft flying. One telling comment is reported to have come from former Air Vice-Marshall 'Boz' Robinson, who claimed the MoD was 'trying to do a full pint job with half pint resources'!

Just when the RAF will see the potent MRA.4 in full squadron service remains a matter of conjecture, and whether a literal 'handful' of Super-Nimrods will be able to undertake the tasking currently being levied on an entire fleet of aging aircraft remains to be seen. The spectre of the AEW Nimrod and its hideous developmental costs for no outcome perhaps haunts the MRA.4 programme, only time will tell whether it will be a resounding success.

Below: *Nimrod MR.1 XV250, 201 Squadron summer 1977 displaying unit motif. This shows a slight variation to that shown on MR.1 XZ282.*

Bottom: *Nimrod MR.1 XZ285, 42 Squadron based at RAF St.Mawgan, recorded at Malta on 28th September 1978 displaying unit motif.*

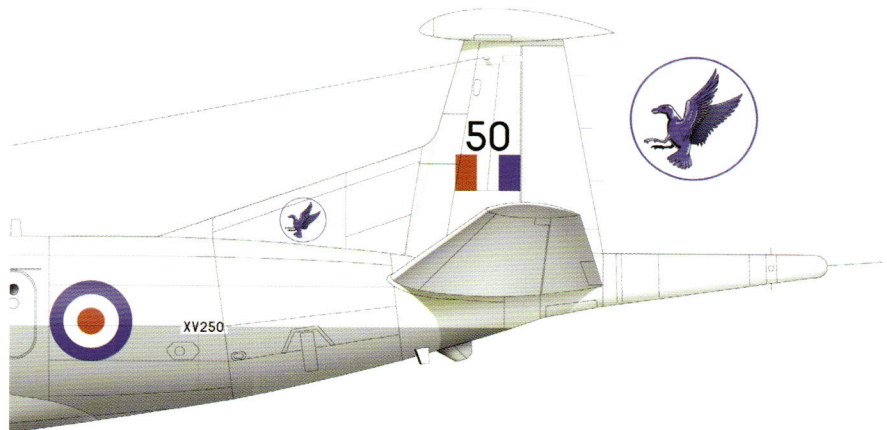

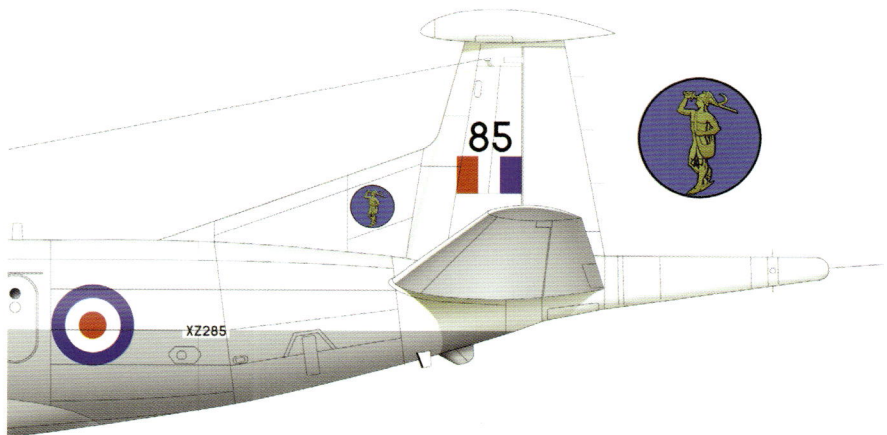

Appendix III: **NIMROD PRODUCTION**

Serial No.	Const. No.	Delivered as	Notes
XV147	06476	MR.1(mod)	Modified from Comet 4C. Fuselage scrapped at Woodford 3/03.
XV148	06477	MR.1(mod)	Modified from Comet 4C. Final flight 1982 to Woodford. Fuselage later scrapped.
XV226	8001	MR.1	Converted to MR.2. Currently with KMRW.
XV227	8002	MR.1	Converted to MR.2. Arrived Woodford 1/7/07 for MRA.4 conversion.
XV228	8003	MR.1	Converted to MR.2. Currently with KMRW.
XV229	8004	MR.1	Converted to MR.2. Currently with KMRW.
XV230	8005	MR.1	Converted to MR.2. KMRW. Crashed Afghanistan 9/06.
XV231	8006	MR.1	Converted to MR.2. Currently with KMRW.
XV232	8007	MR.1	Converted to MR.2. Currently with KMRW.
XV233	8008	MR.1	Converted to MR.2. MoD(PE)/BAE Systems for conversion to MRA.4 ZJ520 (PA-7).
XV234	8009	MR.1	Converted to MR.2. MoD(PE)/BAE Systems for conversion to MRA.4 ZJ518 (PA-2). Arrived Woodford 2/12/99.
XV235	8010	MR.1	Converted to MR.2. Currently with KMRW.
XV236	8011	MR.1	Converted to MR.2. Currently with KMRW.
XV237	8012	MR.1	Converted to MR.2. Broken up 1992 for spares.
XV238	8013	MR.1	Converted to MR.2. Scrapped 1991.
XV239	8014	MR.1	Converted to MR.2. Stalled and crashed 2/9/95 into Lake Ontario, Toronto.
XV240	8015	MR.1	Converted to MR.2. Currently with KMRW.
XV241	8016	MR.1	Converted to MR.2. Currently with KMRW.
XV242	8017	MR.1	Converted to MR.2. MoD(PE)/BAE Systems for conversion to MRA.4 ZJ517 (PA-3).
XV243	8018	MR.1	Converted to MR.2. Delivered to Woodford 27/4/06. For conversion to MRA.4.
XV244	8019	MR.1	Converted to MR.2. Currently with KMRW.
XV245	8020	MR.1	Converted to MR.2. Delivered to Woodford 8/05. For conversion to MRA.4.
XV246	8021	MR.1	Converted to MR.2. Currently with KMRW.
XV247	8022	MR.1	Converted to MR.2. MoD(PE)/BAE Systems for conversion MRA.4 ZJ516 (PA-1). Arrived Woodford 23/11/99.
XV248	8023	MR.1	Converted to MR.2. Currently with KMRW.
XV249	8024	MR.1	Converted to MR.2. Converted to R.1 in 1996 to replace XW666. Currently with 51 Sqn at Waddington
XV250	8025	MR.1	Converted to MR.2. Currently with KMRW.
XV251	8026	MR.1	Converted to MR.2. MoD(PE)/BAE Systems to be converted to MRA.4 ZJ514 (PA-4). Arrived Woodford 26/4/00.
XV252	8027	MR.1	Converted to MR.2. Currently with KMRW.
XV253	8028	MR.1	Converted to MR.2. Became 9118M at Kinloss 11/91. Subsequently scrapped.
XV254	8029	MR.1	Converted to MR.2. Currently with KMRW.
XV255	8030	MR.1	Converted to MR.2. Currently with KMRW.
XV256	8031	MR.1	Converted to MR.2. Crashed 17/11/80 in Roseisle Forest Kinloss. Bird strike, three engines lost and crash ensued.
XV257	8032	MR.1	Converted to MR.2. Weapons bay fire 3/6/84. Scrapped 1992.
XV258	8033	MR.1	Converted to MR.2. MoD(PE)/BAE Systems for conversion to MRA.4 ZJ515 (PA-5). Arrived Woodford 8/11/99
XV259	8034	MR.1	Converted to AEW.3P. Sold for scrap 10/91. Nose section preserved at Solway Aviation Museum, Carlisle. Fuselage GIA Chattenden.
XV260	8035	MR.1	Converted to MR.2. Currently with KMRW.
XV261	8036	MR.1	Converted to AEW.3. Became 8986M. For spares recovery 12/87. Scrapped 1995.
XV262	8037	MR.1	Converted to AEW.3. Struck off charge 12/87. Scrapped Abingdon 06/92.
XV263	8038	MR.1	Converted to AEW.3. 7/87 at Finningley. Fuselage arrived at Woodford from Bournemouth 15/5/02. Nose section at BAE Systems/Warton.
XW664	8039	R.1	51 Sqn. Noted at NAS Patuxent River Washington 17/4/03 to 4/5/03 testing 'Project Extract' systems.
XW665	8040	R.1	51 Sqn Waddington.
XW666	8041	R.1	Ditched 16/5/95 into Moray Firth. Wreck salvaged for spares.
XZ280	8042	MR.1	Converted to AEW.3P. Scrapped 4/92.
XZ281	8043	MR.1	Converted to AEW.3. Scrapped 11/91.
XZ282	8044	MR.1	Converted to AEW.3. 8/89 became 9000M at Kinloss and scrapped by 03/96.
XZ283	8045	MR.1	Converted to AEW.3P. Scrapped 11/91.
XZ284	8046	MR.2	Converted to MR.2 MoD(PE)/BAE Systems for conversion to MRA.4 ZJ519 (PA-6). Arrived Woodford 8/00.
XZ285	8047	MR.1	Converted to AEW.3 Struck off charge 5/92. Scrapped.
XZ286	8048	–	For AEW.3 programme. Struck off charge 12/87. RAF Kinloss fire section (8968M) Scrapped.
XZ287	8049	–	For AEW.3 programme. Became 9140M FCR Stafford 9140M.
ZJ514	PA-04	MRA.4	MoD(PE)/BAE Systems. Conversion of XV251.
ZJ515	PA-05	MRA.4	MoD(PE)/BAE Systems. Conversion of XV258.
ZJ516	PA-01	MRA.4	MoD(PE)/BAE Systems Conversion of XV247. Made its maiden flight from BAE Systems/ Woodford on 26/8/04.

Serial No.	Const. No.	Delivered as	Notes
ZJ517	PA-03	MRA.4	MoD(PE)/BAE Systems Conversion of XV242. Noted at Woodford 6/05. Made its maiden flight on 29/8/05 at Woodford. Returned to BAE Warton 15/12/05 after being painted at Norwich.
ZJ518	PA-02	MRA.4	MoD(PE)/BAE Systems Conversion of XV234. Arrived Warton 15/12/04. Returned to Woodford 13/1/05.
ZJ519	PA-06	MRA.4	MoD(PE)/BAE Systems. Conversion of XZ284
ZJ520	PA-07	MRA.4	MoD(PE)/BAE Systems. Conversion of XV233
ZJ521	PA-08	MRA.4	
ZJ522	PA-09	MRA.4	
ZJ523	PA-10	MRA.4	
ZJ524	PA-11	MRA.4	
ZJ525	PA-12	MRA.4	
ZJ526	PA-13	MRA.4	Cancelled 7/04
ZJ527	PA-14	MRA.4	Cancelled 7/04
ZJ528	PA-15	MRA.4	Cancelled 7/04
ZJ529	PA-16	MRA.4	Cancelled 7/04
ZJ530	PA-17	MRA.4	Cancelled 7/04
ZJ531	PA-18	MRA.4	Cancelled 7/04
ZJ532	PA-19	MRA.4	Cancelled 3/02
ZJ533	PA-20	MRA.4	Cancelled 3/02
ZJ534	PA-21	MRA.4	Cancelled 3/02

AEW.3 programme airframe cross reference

DB1	XZ286	P1	XZ285	P4	XZ283	P7	XV262
DB2	XZ287	P2	XV259	P5	XZ280	P8	XV261
DB3	XZ281	P3	XV263	P6	XZ282		

PRODUCTION SUMMARY

Version	Quantity	Assembly Location	Order Completed
HS.801 prototypes	2 conversions	Chester	1964-07/67
Nimrod MR.1	38	Woodford	1967-08/72
Nimrod R.1	3	Woodford	1970-1973
Nimrod MR.1	8	Woodford	1973-1975
Nimrod MR.2	35 conversions	Woodford	1978-mid 1984
Nimrod AEW.3	11 conversions	Woodford	1979-1984
Nimrod R.1	1 conversion	Woodford	10/95-12/96

TECHNICAL DATA

Nimrod MR1

Length:	126ft 9ins (38.63m)
Wing-span:	114ft 10in (35.00m)
Height:	30ft (9.1m) to tip of tail
Max Speed:	575mph (926km/h)
Engines:	Four Rolls-Royce Spey 250/1 turbofans
Ceiling:	44,000ft (13,405m)
Armament:	Includes Sidewinder AIM-9, Harpoon, 9 x Mark 46 or Stingray Torpedoes

Nimrod MR.2

Length:	126ft 9ins (38.63m)
Wing-span:	114ft 10ins (35.00m)
Height:	30ft (9.1m) to tip of tail
Max Speed:	575mph (926km/h)
Engines:	Four Rolls-Royce Spey 251 turbofans
Ceiling:	44,000ft (13,405m)
Armament:	Includes Sidewinder AIM-9, Harpoon, 9 x Mark 46 or Stingray Torpedoes

Nimrod R1

Length:	117ft 8ins (35.86m)
Wing-span:	114ft 10in (35.00m)
Height:	30ft (9.1m) to tip of tail
Max Speed:	575mph (926km/h)
Engines:	Four Rolls-Royce Spey 251 turbofans
Ceiling:	44,000ft (13,405m)

Nimrod AEW

Length:	137ft 9ins (41.97m)
Wing-span:	114ft 10in (35.00m)
Height:	30ft (9.1m) to tip of tail
Max Speed:	575mph (926Km/h)
Engines:	Four Rolls-Royce Spey 250/1 turbofans
Ceiling:	44,000ft (13,405m)
Armament:	None

Nimrod MRA4

Length:	126ft 9ins (38.63m)
Wing-span:	127ft (38.7m)
Height:	30ft (9.1m) to tip of tail
Max Speed:	mach 0.77
Engines:	Four BMW Rolls-Royce BR710
Ceiling:	44,000ft (13,405m)
Armament:	Includes Sidewinder AIM-9, Harpoon, 9 x Mark 46 or Stingray Torpedoes. See text

ABBREVIATIONS/GLOSSARY

AAR	Air-to-Air Refuelling
ACS	Armament Control System
AEW	Airborne Early Warning
ALARM	Air Launched Anti-Radar Missile
AMRAAM	Advanced Medium Range Air-to-Air Missile
ASR	Air Staff Requirement
ASRAAM	Advanced Short Range Air-to-Air Missile
AST	Air Staff Target
ASTOR	Airborne Stand Off Radar
ASW	Anti Submarine Warfare
ATARM	Advanced Tactical Anti-Radar Missile
ATMI	Airborne Moving Target Indicator
AWACS	Airborne Warning And Control System
CAD	Computer Aided Design
COMINT	Communications Intelligence
COTS	Commercial Off The Shelf
DASS	Defensive Aids Sub-System
ECM	Electronic Countermeasures
ELINT	Electronic Intelligence
ESM	Electronic Support Measures
FASS	Fore and Aft Scanner System
Flt Lt	Flight Lieutenant
FMICW	Frequency-Modulated Intermittent Continuous-Wave
IFF	Identification Friend of Foe
IFR	In-Flight Refuelling
JTU	Joint Trials Unit
LORAN	Long Range Aerial Navigation

MAD	Magnetic Anomaly Detector
Maverick	anti-armour air-to-surface missile
MOD	Ministry Of Defence (UK)
MOD PE	Ministry Of Defence Procurement Executive (UK)
MR	Maritime Reconnaissance
MRA	Maritime Reconnaissance Attack
MSA	Mission System Avionics
NATO	North Atlantic Treaty Organisation
OCU	Operational Conversion Unit
RAF	Royal Air Force
RWR	Radar Warning Receiver
SAR	Search and Rescue
SAR	Synthetic Aperture Radar
SAS	Special Air Service
SATCOM	Satellite Communications
Sgt	Sergeant
SIGINT	Signals Intelligence
SLAM–ER	Stand off Land Attack Missile – Expanded Response
Storm Shadow – cruise missile	
TACAN	Tactical Air Navigation
TEZ	Total Exclusion Zone
TRD	Towed Radar Decoy
UHF	Ultra High Frequency
UN	United Nations
VHF	Very High Frequency
Wg Cdr	Wing Commander

A Nimrod is always on standby at RAF Kinloss, 24 hours a day, 365 days a year. RAF